UNWAVERING HONOR

JIM CALAMS

With Lisa Bell

To all the people who always believed in me, stood by me, and mentored me in reaching my ultimate goal—to become a police officer. I am truly thankful to every one of you. To all my brothers and sisters in blue, we ensured that each of our communities were a safer place to live.

Jim Calams

Table of Contents

Acknowledgments vii

Introducing Jim Calams 1

First Day at South Mountain Precinct................... 16

Hostage Situation... 27

The Sands of Iwo Jima Incident 32

4Sam24 37

Shooting on the Black Canyon Freeway 45

911 Hang up 53

Don't Lie About Me... 60

The Los Angeles Police Academy—my First Hours,
O Dark Thirty 72

Just Beat It... 81

1994 Northridge Earthquake 104

The Day We Cornered OJ 117

Plane Crash—Pacific Division 129

Reflections 135

About the Author... 146

Acknowledgments

My parents, Tim and Kay Calams, who always supported me, encouraged, and guided me to achieve my goals.

My wife D'Ann Calams, who encouraged me and helped me study for tests. I would have never graduated from the academy without her.

George Meier who always took the time to talk to me and guide me in the right direction to fulfill my career as a law enforcement officer.

Additionally, Jerry VanHeldebrecht, my criminal justice professor, who instilled in me first hand to "Never Quit, Never."

Lastly, Mark Beadles, my first training officer, who pushed me to the limits to ensure I was prepared to survive the streets.

I love each of you.

Introducing Jim Calams

A typical, freezing New Year's Eve in Chicago, Illinois, Timothy and Catherine Calams welcomed me into the world.

The youngest of three children, my parents took me home after a brief hospital stay, where my sister, Christine, and brother, Timothy John Calams, waited. During my childhood, we lived in the same house on Chestnut Street, a post WWII home my parents purchased in Des Plaines, Illinois. The modest three-bedroom single family home with one bathroom and a basement sat beside the SOO Line railroad tracks. Only 180 feet from the back of our house, the trains rumbled down the tracks daily with an ear-splitting roar and the horn blaring.

My life, referred to by all in my family as the "baby," was the typical blue collar upbringing. My hard-working father, a veteran of WWII, served in the U.S. Army Air Corps. He worked for the phone company as a cable installer. Later in his career, he became a supervisor, mentoring and training new employees.

My mother, Catherine—known as Kay to all her family and friends—took care of our household. She also worked at Sears Roebuck as an installation writer, sending technicians to homes for new installations.

We only had one car that my dad drove 20 miles to downtown Chicago every day for his job. Mom took a bus to work. I remember her telling me, "James, I have to always keep quarters handy." That's what a one-way bus trip to her job in Des Plaines cost.

Every day, my mom walked to the corner to catch her bus. Sun, rain, snow, wind—she braved it all. Even if we bought a second car, my mom never learned how to drive, and she didn't want to learn. She told me she didn't have the patience to drive, even though at one time or another, each of us encouraged her to learn. Her choice, and we all respected it. Instead, over the years, we watched as she withstood various weather conditions and disappeared into the doorway of public transportation. She never complained.

My sister, brother, and I attended a Catholic grade school. As Greek descendants, my grandparents wanted my sister and brother to attend "Greek school." No matter how much they tried, my mother would not agree. Dad and she came to an agreement for all of us to attend St. Stephens Grade School in Des Plaines.

As the youngest, I attended the school for eight years. We wore uniforms, and they didn't exactly scream style. Green cotton button-up collared shirts—not so bad. Paired with a red tie, questionable choice. Our pants had to be black, and black dress shoes finished the look. Never jeans, t-shirts, and tennis shoes, we wore the same outfit daily.

The nuns served as our teachers, and boy were they brutal. They taught in the mid-1960s to 1970s with a firm hand, ruler, yardstick, and paddle—along with a voice so intimidating they didn't need the other objects often.

Even though I never served in the military, I used to make light of it later in life as being in Marine Corps Boot Camp for eight years. I respect the Corps immensely, as I have several friends and police partners who were in that branch of the military. Listening to their stories reminded me of the nuns at St. Stephens. Tougher than any drill sergeant, they didn't take anything from us kids, and normally, we didn't try to give them any trouble, either.

While in grade school, one of the nuns assigned me to "Patrol Duty." Wow. I beamed and went home, saying, "I'm a patrol boy now. I get to cross people, and cars have to stop." So much power in a child, and I loved it. How many kids get to command a car to stop before they hit puberty? I did this for several years before and after school.

They added a bright orange vinyl strap that went over one side of your shoulder on top of the standard uniform issue. The other side came around your waist and secured there. Once you finished daily patrols, you rolled this safety device into the size of a baseball and looped it through your pants belt. It made you look cool—at least I thought it did.

Looking back now, that was my first Duty Rig—a belt around the waist that holds everything a police officer might need while on duty. Even as a young boy, I had foreshadowing of a police lifestyle.

During my school years, I played baseball

in my free time. When summer arrived, I started out with the Stars of Tomorrow, Little League, Pony League, and then later went on to play high school ball. I thrived in team sports, learning discipline, and skills for working with others.

I always wanted to be a professional baseball player, but that never happened. Instead, it instilled my team player attitude for everything I did later in life, up to and including today. Few make it in the world of professional sports, but the smart ones learn from the experience and transfer those soft skills to whatever they do.

Some people go through life and never know what they want to do or be. They take a job that pays bills but don't consider what they honestly want. Some may discover in college or later what they desire most. That wasn't the case for me. I always knew I wanted to protect and serve. I wanted to be that person who is there for other people. Initially, I thought I needed to go into the military first, then pursue my lifelong ambition of becoming a police officer. I neared the end of high school with a plan.

My godmother, Barbara Meier, was

married to a Cook County Deputy Sheriff named George Meier. A giant of a man, he stood at least six-foot-four and weighed 235 pounds. I always had to look up to him literally—figuratively, he earned it. He was so much taller than me back in my pre-teen days.

George knew I wanted to become a police officer, and he always took time to talk to me about the rewards of the job but also the dangers that went with it. I was very proud of George and what he stood for. He subsequently went on to be a bodyguard and driver for the sheriff back in the 1970s, involved in major cases, including the investigation of the monster, John Wayne Gacy.

Although George couldn't say much about ongoing cases, his facial expressions revealed those that tore at his heart. Gacy's monstrous murder of more than 30 boys and young men haunted him. The perp's obvious lack of remorse made that horrendous case worse. No cop wants such a horrific case, but choosing the life of a police officer opens the door to one case that won't let you go.

When I was 21, we were playing a game of billiards in his basement. I mentioned to George the frustration I felt, trying to get an interview and even make a hiring list with some of the agencies I tested for.

He looked at me, and with his calm voice and a smile, he said, "You'll get there. Just keep trying."

His words fueled my determination. I idn't give up. More than anything, I wanted to nor his faith in me. When I doubted myself, words replayed in my thoughts. "You'll get re."

I did, George. Rest in peace, Hero.

∞∞∞∞∞∞∞

My best friend Kevin Wilkens, who I me friends with in high school, was a tall well-defined person. A wrestler in high l, he was very vigilant when he wrestled.

evin, like his brother Leon, decided he wanted to go into the United States Army upon graduation from high school. Now, I think Kevin's father had some influence on his joining the military. At least, that's the impression I got after hanging out at his house several times. It seemed like a good idea to me. If my best friend planned to join, maybe I should too.

I went through the process of joining the

Army, took the tests, and the physical exam. I told the recruiter I wanted to be in the Military Police and waited for the Army's response.

Before long, the recruiter called. I picked up the receiver of the wall-mounted landline telephone at my house, wondering and excited about the potential.

He said, "You're in luck. I got you into MP school, 95 Charlie."

"95 Charlie. Great." I didn't know exactly what that meant, and I didn't ask, assuming that must be Army code for becoming a MP.

Later, in May 1975, Kevin Wilkens's brother, Leon, returned home after serving as a MP in Germany. I looked forward to hearing about his experiences, so I headed over to their house.

Leon said, "Hey, I hear you're going into the Army."

"Yes, I am."

"What's your MOS?"

That one I knew. Military Occupational Specialties. I beamed. "95 Charlie."

Leon laughed. He stopped, caught his breath, and laughed some more. I didn't see anything funny.

"What?"

Leon shook his head. "Jim, 95 Charlie means you'll be working the prisons. AKA prison guard. It's just horrible duty. Man, they suckered you."

"Oh no. That can't be right." I clenched my jaw, trying to stay cool but feeling a mixture of embarrassment and anger over my naivety. "That recruiter told me I'll be a patrolling MP."

"Patrolling the prison, maybe. I hate to tell you this, Jim, but he lied to you. They always lie. It gets their quota filled. By the time most kids find out the truth—too late."

I heard enough. "Thanks for telling me, Leon."

Not sure whether I could fix this mess, I called the recruiter the next day and fronted him out. "Is 95 Charlie working in the prison?"

"Who told you that?" No denial, no confirmation. But his tone told me I nailed him.

"I changed my mind." I had no intention of letting him get away with the lie and throw me into a job I didn't want instead of one to prepare me for the future I dreamed of all my life.

I'm here to tell you, that guy called my house every day for two weeks. Finally, my dad got fed up with the recruiter interrupting our family dinners. He told him to quit calling, and after that, the calls ceased.

One day, my dad turned to me and said, "You can go out and get a job. Maybe I can get you a position at the phone company. Or you can go to school."

I opted for school.

At Oakton Community College, located in Morton Grove, Illinois, I registered for Administration of Justice and Criminal Justice classes. I also took on a part-time job for a company that moved furniture for big stores like Sears and Montgomery Wards. Not my first choice, but it could meet my needs while I went to school.

I thought, "Here I go, learning about police work and our justice system."

The first class I attended was Police Procedures. Nineteen years old, I walked into this classroom, and all I saw were police officers—off duty, wearing guns on their hips. Some had shoulder holsters.

Man, those guys were cocky.

All of them looked at me when I walked in. They fell silent, but the looks on their faces screamed, "What the fuck is this young punk doing here?"

If they meant to intimidate me, it worked. I kept quiet and listened to the teacher, Jerry VanHeldebrecht, who later became a mentor of mine.

Jerry was a retired police detective with all kinds of experience in the Chicago area. I used to stay after class and ask his advice on many subjects pertaining to my studies and applying for police agencies in the area. He always had time for me, claiming I reminded him of himself when he first started in police work.

He didn't sugarcoat anything for me. "Getting into this field is hard. There's a lot of competition. A multitude of applicants battling for a handful of jobs."

Boy, was he right.

As time passed, I put in applications for several police departments in the Chicago area. Time after time, I seldom landed an interview after taking the tests. When I eventually got a few interviews, they didn't end with an employment offer.

I wondered whether I had what it took to become a police officer. These obstacles didn't fit the plan for my life. In a mental state of failure, I took my concerns to Jerry and told him what I was feeling.

He looked at me and said, "Calams, quitting at something should never be an option. You never quit." He paused, his eyes boring into my soul. "Never quit, Calams. Never!"

After hearing his words—really hearing him—this man I admired and trusted completely looking straight into my eyes, something came over me. *This man knows I can do it, and I know I can do it. So, screw it! I'm going to keep going back 'til I reach my goal.*

Jerry's words stuck with me throughout the rest of my life, and although he gave me that wisdom first, it wasn't the last time I'd hear the same thing. From the beginning, I learned that honor can never waver, and perseverance counts most when you feel like quitting. Never give up became part of me.

My parents retired and moved to Tucson, Arizona in 1981. I stayed in Illinois, working a meaningless job just to make ends meet, but I kept taking police tests.

Throughout the nation, the job economy at

that time stank. The last test I took in Illinois was for the Arlington Heights PD. Over one thousand people took that test for four positions. I couldn't help thinking, "I would have better luck trying out for the Green Berets."

There, with a few friends, we looked at each other. A single expression between us summed it up without a word. *This is just ridiculous. Impossible.* We left, silent and without much hope.

I kept in constant communication with my parents, and they encouraged me to move out to Arizona and test there. It didn't take much convincing. In 1982, I packed my meager belongings in my green Jeep CJ7 and drove to Tucson.

When I arrived at their home, I was about to pass out. "102 freaking degrees! Oh my God. This is terrible. How do these folks stand this?"

"Oh, it's a dry heat. You'll get used to it." Everyone I encountered had the same standard response.

I got right to it and took a job at Oshman's Sporting Goods selling firearms. At least it was a fun job. I met some very nice employees and customers, but it didn't pay shit—about $3.25 an hour.

My parents saw a recruitment poster in the newspaper. The Maricopa County Sheriff's office was in town, giving tests for Detention Officer. I thought back to my outrage over the Army recruiter who tried to place me as a prison guard. I still didn't want that kind of job.

Then I remembered, one time after being denied for yet another position, I asked a police officer why.

He looked at me and stated, "You don't have any experience."

That just made me pissed. "Well, how do I get experience if you won't hire me?"

He laughed. "I hear you, but because we can be so selective with who we hire, that's just the way it is for you right now."

"So, how do I get experience?"

"Working in a jail is a good start. Not what you want, but we look at applicants in that field."

At the time, I didn't like the answer. With a possibility of working for Maricopa County before me, it felt like perhaps a way into the career of my dreams.

I took the MCSO test, passed, and had an interview the very next day. They set up my psychological test and physical exams. I passed all of them, and they offered me a job.

I had been dating my sweetheart, D'Ann. When I asked her to marry me, she accepted, and we married on October 29, 1983.

Finally, headed in the right direction, we moved to the Phoenix area one week later and rented an apartment.

No longer feeling like a failure, I had the love of my life with me and moved a step in the right direction toward a new career—the one I wanted from before I became a Patrol Boy in grade school.

Eventually, that opening led to becoming a police officer, complete with attending the police academy and moving to a position on the streets of Arizona.

That's where the rest of my story began.

First Day at South Mountain Precinct

I graduated from the police academy in November 1985, the same night our first-born daughter, Stephanie, was born. The tiny, perfect image of beauty stole my breath. My wife and I celebrated, ecstatic to welcome her to our family.

Fortunately, I had a few days off prior to reporting for my first shift. The day shift ran 0600-1600 (6:00 a.m.-4:00 p.m.), on duty Tuesday and Wednesday with Thursday off.

That morning I kissed my wife goodbye, leaving her half-asleep with our newborn. Despite the night of interrupted sleep every new parent experiences, my energy level soared. I left the house, bouncing toward my car, breathless with anticipation. After so many years of trying, I finally reached my goal of becoming a police officer and was super pumped to get to my duty station.

I showed up through the front door early with my uniform and duty gear already on. Veteran cops, the old timers, the outspoken, all turned to stare at me.

One shouted, "Hey we got us a new rookie here."

I looked at him and smiled, hiding my thoughts of fuck off asshole. I continued through the station's corridor.

One officer approached. "Who you looking for?"

"Sergeant Ramsey, sir." The confidence inside spilled into my voice.

"Sir." The officer laughed. "I guess I got promoted." He smiled and motioned for me to follow him.

We entered the sergeant's office. "John, he's one of yours." Turning to me, he said, "He'll take good care of you."

I extended my hand to shake his.

"Welcome aboard. I'm Conrad Anderson, but they call me Connie."

"Thanks, Connie."

In the office, Sergeant John Ramsey, a veteran of the department, looked at me. "Have a seat." He never cracked a smile, all business, and continued with his expectations of me and who would train me.

"Officer Calams—and I say that lightly right now—this is Officer Beadles. He will be training you on our squad. You do what he says. Do you understand me?"

"Yes, sir. I understand." If I had an ounce of cockiness in me, it dissipated at that moment. However, the confidence and enthusiasm remained strong.

I shook Ramsey's hand and followed behind Officer Beadles like a barely weaned puppy following its master.

Officer Beadles spoke without looking back at me. "I'm a veteran of the United States Marine Corps. Were you in the Corps?"

"No, sir, I was not."

"Figures."

I didn't know how to respond to that, so I kept quiet.

Beadles was a strapping guy, 6' 3", 225 pounds, very confident of himself. I could tell this guy was going to be more than demanding of me.

He sat me down, and we went over paperwork before he presented me with a binder and other items I needed to use during my training. I only thought graduating from the academy completed my preparation for becoming a police officer.

After receiving the paperwork and binder, but not with a second to look at the contents, we went out to the police parking lot to get our patrol car. Much to my surprise, Beadles led me to a 1979 Dodge Aspen. Filthy inside, it stank of cigarettes, and massive amounts of spent sunflower-seed shells littered the floor boards.

Beadles wrinkled his nose, shuddering. "You see how this car looks? I never want to see you do this. You understand me?"

"Yes, sir, I understand." The stench and mess made my stomach churn. He didn't need to worry about me leaving a patrol car like that. Ever.

We went over the components — siren, lights, PA speakers, and the MDT, which was an on-board computer. Nice, although somewhat already antiquated in 1985.

Beadles continued to talk about the functions of the car, then he pulled out a pack of Red Marlboro cigarettes, pulled one out of the hard box and lit it up.

"You smoke?"

"No, sir."

"Too bad. I do, but I'll keep the window open for you."

"That's fine, sir." I wondered if he normally used that car and whether the sunflower seed shells belonged to him alongside the odor. I didn't ask.

"There's one thing you need to know about me. They call me the axe man."

"OK." I sat there listening to this guy, and I figured I'd ask him. Swallowing hard, I said, "So, I have to ask. Why do they call you the axe man?"

"Because I wash out people who can't hack this job."

I stared at him, considering my words carefully. Finally, I licked my lips. "I will work as hard as I have to and prove to you who I am and what I can do." I had no intention of letting this guy defeat and wash me out when I worked so hard and long to get there.

A smirk grew on his lips. "That's fine. We will see."

Officer Mark Beadles pushed me in every direction, some I didn't know were possible to push. We took report calls from other officers. We responded to different sides of the precinct to handle calls.

"You hear a call go out and nobody answers it, you better be answering it and responding to the call. Are we clear?"

"Yes, sir, very clear."

As my training progressed, whenever I submitted any handwritten reports worded incorrectly, he made me do them over. Any of my tactics in question, he corrected me on the spot, but he also made notes of every error.

Exhausted by the end of my shifts with this guy, I saw other people I graduated with from the academy. Laughing, drinking coffee, chatting with their training officers—not me. I had the commandant of the Marine Corps. Without a basis for comparison, I felt sure basic training for the Corps might have been easier.

We continued with my training at warp speed, handling over 35 radio calls per shift. We averaged 10 departmental reports of burglary, theft, and traffic accidents, along with aggravated and misdemeanor assaults. We wrote traffic citations galore. Beadles' aspirations of being a motorcycle officer were evident with the enforcement of traffic law.

During early spring 1986, my training neared completion. One thing Beadles always did—he answered calls near the end of our shift. These calls often came from the other officers busy "circling the wagons."

Beadles mentioned to me several times, "We answer because some officers are ready to go home and aren't adhering to 'beat responsibility.'"

He drummed that into my head.

One day toward the end of our shift, we kept getting a broadcast from the radio dispatcher. "Any unit to meet the detectives at 35th Avenue and Dobbins Road for a possible suicide of a burned body?"

Beadles grabbed the mic. "4Adam12. We will handle the call. Show us en route."

As we pulled up to a desolate area of the desert, we saw the detectives waving us over.

One detective walked toward us. "Hey Mark, good to see you. Who's this?"

"Rocky, this is my trainee, Jim Calams."

"Nice to meet you kid. How you like it so far?"

"I like it a lot, sir."

"Ha. Sir." He chuckled. "I'm a working cop. You can call me Rocky."

"Nice to meet you, Rocky."

"Ever see a burned body before, Jim?"

"No, I can't say that I have." As I walked toward the human remains, the smell assailed my nose—horrendous stench I still can't describe, but one I can't forget. The body lay on the ground, curled tightly in a fetal like position.

"Looks like a suicide to us," Rocky said.

I started the standard process, getting the names and serial numbers of all the personnel on the scene, recording them on my field interrogation card. Looking around, I noticed something that struck me as odd.

A set of footprints appeared in the general area, pointing away from the body. My crime-scene training kicked in. First rule—never contaminate an area in any way. Secure the area if necessary.

I followed those footprints a good 25 yards toward a raised brim of desert. Words written in the dirt stopped me cold. "You bitch."

I walked back over to the crime scene. *OK, this is some weird shit. This has to be related to the call we're on.*

Beadles' voice broke my thoughts. "Where the hell have you been?"

"Hey, Mark. I don't think this is a suicide."

All the personnel on the scene snickered at the rookie.

I got pissed. I had something, and they just laughed. Pushing down the anger, I refused to let them deter me. "No, I found something that makes me question suicide."

Beadles studied my face, then came up to me. "Show me what you're talking about."

I took Beadles and Rocky over to the area where I found the words.

They peered down at the writing and then at each other. "You just might have something here, Jim," Detective Rocky said.

The crime-scene technicians arrived and proceeded taking pictures of the area, including the footprints left with the words, processing every possible bit of evidence in the area.

We watched for several minutes before Beadles tapped me. "OK, let's let these guys finish up here. Let's head into the barn (police jargon for let's go home)."

A few days passed before Beadles received a phone call from Detective Rocky. They were pursuing the son of the burned body victim as a suspect. "It's a homicide, Mark. Tell your trainee good work."

Beadles looked at me with a slow smile. "Now that's police work. Good job." He recorded in my training binder about my persistence and attention to details.

Finally, I got his attention. On cloud nine, I cherished those notes. My first homicide. I stood a little taller that day.

During my time at the academy, one of our instructors told us, "Sometimes, you just have to follow your gut out there in the streets." It worked that time. I followed my gut, and it paid off in justice for the victim.

Soon after that, the time came for Beadles to put me out on my own—going solo.

Mark looked at me, shook my hand and said, "I was really hard on you because I want you to be safe and successful in your job. I know I pissed you off, but it's my job to make sure you are ready." He paused for only a moment. "You're ready, Jim."

To this day, I have to say Mark Beadles remains a very good friend of mine. Later in my career as a police officer, I used some of Mark's training methods to train new police officers. In the same way he made me angry sometimes, they got pissed at me. I didn't care. Their safety and success meant more than a popularity contest. They didn't need to like me—they needed to learn the job and walk away from encounters safe and proud of the job they did.

During our training, Mark Beadles always discussed how he wanted to be a motorcycle officer and how he loved to ride them. He finally achieved his goal of becoming a motor officer—a very fine one, I might add.

John "Rambo" Ramsey, my first supervisor in police work, also became a good friend. He subsequently transferred to court services. Five years later, when I told him I was leaving to join the Los Angeles Police Department, he looked at me and said, "We always lose the good ones."

Fighting back a tear because he thought that highly of me, I shook his hand, thanked him, and said goodbye.

Hostage Situation

In the South Mountain Police district of Phoenix, the sun thrashed the earth, hot air making the simplest breathing feel like opening an oven door without sniffing a tantalizing aroma. Working Shift 2, I received a radio call.

"4Frank12—242."

Great. 242—an assault in progress, possible domestic violence.

Before I could respond, the dispatcher's voice crackled over the radio. "4Frank12, be advised, you are rolling alone. There is no other unit available for backup."

The call came out hot, so I had no time to wait for backup even if I expected it. I arrived within one minute. I parked down the street and rushed toward the home.

An elderly woman intercepted me. "I called the police." Tears ran down her cheeks, her eyes wide. "My son's in the house with a knife. You have to hurry!" She grabbed my arm. "I think he wants to kill his girlfriend."

Right then, sweat poured down my back, the extreme heat of the day pressing against my senses. My heart raced as the beats of my pulse increased, pounding against my temples. Tunnel vision seized me as I looked and then headed toward the front door.

OK, Jim, get it together like you were trained in the academy.

I approached the front door carefully. Deep breath. Vision clearing. I entered the home. Trained tactics took control. I sliced the pie without exposing myself to any open hallway.

Blood-curdling screams hit my ears. Female. Rear of the house. I inhaled, slowing my heart a bit. Entering a three-foot wide hallway, maybe 21 feet long, I noticed the bedroom door—closed. More screaming from inside. Then a male's voice joined the shrieks.

"Shut the fuck up, bitch. You whore."

Bingo! Here's the shithead.

I opened the bedroom door slowly and tactically sliced the pie. Needed a view of my suspect. The screaming continued hysterically from the female. Not escalating. Not calming either. Split second decision. Gotta move.

At the low ready with my Smith and Wesson Model 27, 357 Magnum. Trained tactical stance, I identified myself. "Police Officer."

I pushed the door all the way back.

Thwump!

The door banged against the wall.

What I saw next blew my mind. Not everything you see as a cop looks like the movies. The scene spread before me, surreal. I froze, feeling like an actor in a movie, yet knowing nothing could be more real.

A young Hispanic woman, early twenties, terror-filled eyes. Seated in a chair, bound with duct tape, she looked into my eyes. Panicked, silently begging me to save her.

A male Hispanic, around the same age, crouched behind her. A massive kitchen butcher knife at her throat.

Crap. Not good.

"Get the fuck out, cop. I'm gonna kill this bitch. Then, I'm gonna kill you, mother fucker."

I don't think so, asshole.

I pushed down the adrenaline. Steadied my

five-inch Magnum. Stared him down. Academy tactics' voices returned.

Remember, an assailant can cause serious harm to you within seven feet.

I had at least 12 feet and seconds to decide.

I can see my sights. I see the red ramp sight. OK. I'm ready. Gonna have to be a headshot.

"Get the fuck out, cop. I swear I'll kill you!"

Putting on a loud, commanding voice, I steady myself. "Last chance, pepper gut. Drop the knife."

Dazed by the derogatory term, horror filled his eyes. The knife shook in his hand. Then, the suspect stepped back and away from the bound girlfriend. A moment passed, both of us watching the other.

Would he charge me?

Would I shoot?

Suddenly, he stepped to the side and dropped the knife.

I didn't wait. "Get on your stomach. Face down. Don't move."

He hit the floor. I kicked away the knife and exhaled. The backup I didn't expect arrived at that moment and took the suspect into custody.

Sweat drenched my entire body, my heart

rate still elevated, but decreasing.

While driving back to the station so I could book the suspect, he cowered in the back seat of my patrol car.

Sobbing, he said, "But I love her so much."

He bawled like a baby. Some tough guy.

"You were going to shoot me. I saw your gun."

I didn't bother to respond.

At the station, I placed the suspect in a holding cell.

My sergeant came up to me. "You should have capped that dickhead."

"It was close, but I had to get my mind right one more time. That's when I called him a pepper gut."

"No shit? You called him that? I'm surprised he didn't charge you." He chuckled. "Hey, Jimbo, whatever works. Hurry up and book this guy. We need you out there. Shorthanded tonight."

The Sands of Iwo Jima Incident

Another typical hot desert night, I worked at the South Mountain Precinct in Phoenix, Arizona. That night, Steven Konegni rode along as my partner.

Steven served in the military, a USMC veteran and a tenured police officer with a knack for finding stolen vehicles with occupants still inside. Assigned the walking beat detail, we patrolled the projects in South Phoenix—the Coffelt Apartments, most often referred to as the Coffelts. Built in 1953 for veterans returning from Korea, the county annexed the property in 1959, turning the apartments into low-income housing. In addition to the walking beat, we also handled all radio calls in the area.

Darkness settled over the neighborhood. At approximately 2100 hours (9 p.m.), Steve was running license plates on the MDT (Mobile Data

Transmitter) in our patrol car. Sitting within arm's reach of my partner, I watched the streets and jumped at an outburst from him.

"Jimbo, we have a rollin' stolen right in front of us. Call it out on the radio."

Adrenaline pumped through my veins. As I advised the radio dispatcher of our location and activated the overhead lights, the driver slammed on the brakes. He bailed out the driver's door.

Oh crap. Runner.

"4W44. We are in foot pursuit in the Coffelts," shouted Steven in a firm voice.

Steve was a jackrabbit. Even now, I've never seen anyone run as fast as this guy could. Before I exited the patrol car, Steve was on the suspect.

Known as a very violent area, we regularly worked shootings, drug dealing, child abductions, and of course, stolen vehicles. It was a no-brainer for me to deploy the Remington 870 12-gauge pump shotgun.

My heart raced as I tried to catch up to Steve. We ran through several areas muddled with ruts, jumping cactus bushes, and clotheslines. No streetlights, the pitch blackness threw shadows where nothing stood and hid objects capable of inflicting agony.

Behind Steve approximately 15 yards, he rounded a corner complex. The darkness swallowed everything, blocking Steve from my sight.

Suddenly, Steve's voice broke the silence. "Jimbo, hurry up! He's trying to get my gun."

As I rounded the corner, this massive suspect appeared. Maybe 6'2", he weighed well over 200 pounds. Pulling frantically, he tried to get officer Konegni's Sig 226 9mm from his holster.

Steve's tone turned frantic. "Hurry, Jimbo! Get this asshole off me!"

If the suspect freed my partner's weapon…

I didn't let myself finish the thought.

Remington 870 still in my hands, I took a breath, trying to stay calm. "Steve, turn your head."

"What?"

"Turn your head, buddy."

Steve turned his head, trusting me completely. Using the deployed 870, I butt stroked the suspect in the head.

Whack!

I had to keep him from using deadly force

against my partner.

The suspect fell to the ground like a cold mackerel. I checked him. Still breathing. We handcuffed the suspect, administered first aid, and advised dispatch to roll fire/EMT to our location. They got the pleasure of providing further aid for the suspect.

The fire department transported the suspect to the local ER where a doctor checked him out and released him to our custody. We jointly transported him back to the station for booking into the county jail.

During the interview, we examined officer Konegni's leather holster. Ripped on the side. The suspect never got the gun out, but he did some serious damage to the holster. The side of the suspect's head sported an ugly knot with some nasty bruising.

Most people called it a goose egg. I called it protecting my partner.

After we advised the suspect of his Miranda Rights, we asked if he would answer our questions?

He wasn't very polite or compliant. "I'm not saying shit. I wanted to kill both you mother fuckers. That's all I gotta say."

With the interview ended, we booked the suspect on two felony counts—driving and in control of a stolen vehicle along with aggravated assault on a police officer.

While we were getting ready to go back into service from the jail, I stopped and pulled Steve over to a counter. The Remington 870 shotgun from our trunk rested there—the stock broken in half.

Steve whistled under his breath. "Jimbo, just like the movie *The Sands of Iwo Jima*." As a Marine Corps veteran, he knew that movie intimately. "You remember when John Wayne butt stroked that guy with his M1 Garand?"

I smirked. "I sure do."

We climbed back into the patrol car. "4W44. Show us 10-8." Back in service, we headed out, waiting for our next call.

4Sam24

You're probably wondering what 4Sam24 means? Well, it's the call sign of a police car that patrolled the drug and crime-ridden area of 24th Street and Broadway Road in Phoenix, Arizona.

Over the years, certain tenured officers spent several years on the job, using knowledge of the street urchins in the area. They helped arrest and convict several felony cases. The area was known for violent shootings, drug dealing, rapes, aggravated assaults—the list went on.

Officer Charles Boyd and officer Jeff Nation normally worked that car, which was on our squad during 2100-0700 hours. The overnight shift starting at 9:00 p.m. saw a lot of activity.

I had knowledge of the area because I knew most of those felons prior to my appointment as a Phoenix police officer. In my job as a

Detention Officer with The Maricopa County Sheriff's Office, I interacted with several of the subjects within the county jail system. I knew how they acted and what they would do to anyone in the law enforcement field, if given the chance, to harm them, their loved ones, or family.

These were not nice people.

Personally, I really didn't want to work the area. When I did, I almost always got a complaint from those shitheads. The veteran officers, Boyd and Nation, were like Teflon. Nothing ever seemed to stick to them as far as getting complaints, but for me, any time I worked with one of them while the other one was off, the complaint ended up lodged against me. For whatever reasons—force or name calling—most of them would tell our supervisor we did something wrong.

One night in May 1987, Boyd took a day off.

My sergeant came up to me. "Hey, you're working with Nation tonight."

"Nooooo." I didn't intend for the word to come out so loudly.

The sergeant's eyebrows furrowed. "Why?"

"Because you know as well as I do, every

time you put me out there, I make some great felony arrests. But they turn into excessive uses of force 90% of the time. I'm the one these assholes complain about."

"Why is that?"

"I don't know, but they do."

The sergeant smiled. "Just work with Jeff. He said he only wants to work with you when Boyd is off. OK?"

I sighed. "Alright. I will, but if I get a beef..."

"OK. I know."

I didn't mind working with Jeff, but I didn't want to deal with yet another complaint.

The night started out quiet. We cruised the neighborhood, keeping an eye open for any trouble. The social clubs had a lot of foot traffic, but it appeared for the moment they were all behaving themselves.

Jeff looked at me. "Hey, let's go get a cup." Coffee—a cop's best friend.

"OK. Cool." I was a little tired, and Jeff mentioned he was in court most of the day, so he needed a pick me up.

We went out to Jeff and Chuck's pop spot, which was the Waffle House. They offered free coffee to cops. What a dump. It smelled. Not of food, but of other things. The place was dirty, but it was their spot, so I played along.

After we finished up, Jeff looked at me. "Let's go get us an arrest."

I liked that idea. "OK. Let's go, Jeff."

Back in our area, it seemed like the night grew darker without warning. No street lights. Those shitheads shot them out to hide their dastardly deeds.

As we cruised around the area, we talked about the job—how it was changing. It was not like when Jeff came on. He had over nine years on the job to my two years, so he definitely saw how the times were changing. Police work headed toward a different direction, and we both knew it.

Jeff Nation kept a file with pictures of the area felons, their crimes, and if they were wanted on any warrant. He knew if the detectives wanted to talk to them.

As we patrolled the area, Jeff spontaneously yelled, "Jimbo, pull over quick."

"Why? What's up?" I didn't see anything out of the ordinary.

"That's Leonard Green over there." He

pointed to an individual—a physically buffed out guy. "I believe he is 10-51 (felony warrant). Here. Run him real quick." He handed me an index card.

I placed Green's info in the computer and pressed transmit. Almost immediately, the dispatcher cleared us.

"4Sam24. Copy your 10-51 information."

"10-4, dispatch. Roll us a backup unit. 4Sam24. Show our location now at 25th Street and Broadway, just north." My pulse beat as fast as a rabbit.

"10-4, 4Sam24." Dispatch paused for a second, then continued. "John25. You copy 4Sam24's location?"

"John25. Yes. I'm a ways off. Please advise them."

OK. My buddy, Nick, was rolling. Good. We were both out of the car, running after Green, who bolted the minute we pulled up.

We finally caught up to him, and the fight was on. This guy, big-time prison-yard buffed out, had the strength of at least two normal men. We were both on him but having a hell of a time getting his hands behind his back. Finally able to get him cuffed, the next thing we knew, a crowd gathered, circling the wagons around us. There must have been at least 15 thugs ready to jump us. Words came at us.

"Yeah, get 'em."

"Let's kill these motherfuckers."

More of the same, coming from every direction. My heart rate spiked. Sweating profusely. Droplets popped out on Jeff's forehead. We were in deep.

Without thinking, I cleared leather. My 5-inch Smith & Wesson model 27 357 Magnum handgun fit my hand. At the low ready, I yelled. "Back up, you motherfuckers."

Looking at the thugs, I did my best to hide fear.

One looked at me, a slow smirk growing across his lips. "Yeah, but you only got six bullets."

"But you—you piece of shit. You get the first one." I leveled the big Magnum at him.

He stared me down. Waiting.

One of the thugs shouted, "Let's go! There's more coming."

Code 3. Sirens screamed, growing louder. Heading our way, lights flashed and sirens blared.

"Damn, the calvary is coming. Thank God."
I blew out a breath of relief.

We took Green into custody. He was a homicide suspect and a horrendous dude. As we put the subject into the car, Jeff and I both shook visibly from the adrenaline racing through our bodies. I was glad to survive a situation that could have ended badly for both of us.

While transporting Green to the main jail for booking, he leaned up to the caged screen in our car. "Hey, big man, is that a 44 Magnum you gots?"

"Yeah." I couldn't help smiling in the dark.

"Damn. That would have fucked someone up."

Both Jeff and I laughed about it later. We both knew we came close to having our asses handed to us, although we didn't mention it to each other or any of our fellow officers. We carried the knowledge inside, thankful for those who came to our assistance at the perfect moment.

Like I mentioned earlier in my dealing with the 4Sam24 car, I always ended up with the complaints from thugs in the area. True to form, the guy who wanted to jump us with his merry band of thugs filed a formal complaint against me. Not Jeff. Me. Because I cussed at him. Never mind that he used the same curse word toward me, alongside threats of death.

Some days, it seems we could never win.

"4Sam24. Show us 10-7 (end of watch). Goodnight."

Shooting on the Black Canyon Freeway

During 1987, I was working patrol shift two—1400-2400 hours in the South Mountain Precinct of Phoenix, Arizona.

It was warm that day, pretty much like every day in the Phoenix area. Working the west side of the precinct, 4Frank11 was my call sign. Well into my shift, everything remained fairly quiet. I handled a few GOA calls—gone on arrival—with no complainant or subjects to contact. I could handle a peaceful shift, even with a few meaningless calls.

As I patrolled the southwest area of the precinct at Dobbins Road and 7th Avenue, a call came over my radio.

"All units, be advised. A shooting just occurred in Tempe." Our Phoenix dispatcher's voice sounded a bit shaky. "A 918 subject (mental person) shot a police lieutenant at 48th

Street and the freeway."

Suddenly, my quiet shift shattered.

"Units be advised, the suspect is described as a white male approximately 19-25 years of age. Units be advised, the suspect is armed with the supervisor's handgun and now has taken a hostage on a motorcycle."

I waited for an update. Better description.

"The suspect is now on a motorcycle, forcing the driver with the handgun pointed to the rear of his head, according to a witness. Suspect has entered the Black Canyon Freeway, heading northbound from 48th Street."

"Holy shit," I muttered. "I need to start heading toward the freeway."

The dispatcher continued with updates. "Suspect now at 24th Street, still northbound on Black Canyon." A pause. "Now at 16th Street."

Time to kick it in the ass.

Driving a piece of junk Chevrolet Malibu 6-cylinder, I had the damn thing floored. Oil smoke blowing out the ass end of the car, I checked the rear-view mirror.

"Suspect motorcycle now approaching 7th Street."

Damn! This dude is coming my way.

"4Frank11. Show me responding code 3 to the freeway."

"10-4, 4Frank11."

Lights flashing, siren blaring, I pushed the car as fast as I could. It shuttered and smoked. The steering wheel swayed to the left. I cursed the city at that moment. They could never get these cars fixed. Too old. Lots of miles on them.

I turned the A/C off, trying to gain more power, even though it didn't work worth a shit. Sweating my ass off, my heart thumped against the siren.

Whoop, whoop, whoop.

"Suspect is at 7th Avenue."

The words came across the radio at the same second I pulled up the ramp to enter Black Canyon at 7th Avenue.

Suddenly, one of my law enforcement heroes, the Arizona DPS, appeared right behind the motorcycle.

Shit.

The bike stopped on the shoulder of the northbound lanes. The motorcycle driver jumped over the guard rail. As I rolled in, the DPS officer deployed his shotgun. The suspect leveled a handgun. Wildness covering him, he pointed. Straight at the officer.

Boom. Boom.

Suspect down.

He already shot one police officer. No playing around with this shithead. The DPS officer lowered his shotgun.

The threat over, we cuffed the suspect, even though he had no pulse and wasn't breathing.

As I helped with the crime scene, I ended up taking the witness statement from the motorcycle driver. He shook all over, rightly so, after enduring the ride of his life. He proceeded to tell me how he slowed down by the police car back on 48th Street in Tempe. The next thing he knew, a gun was pointed in his face. The crazed 918 suspect told him to go. Fearing for his life, the driver went.

"Is he dead?" the victim asked.

"Oh, yeah. He's no longer a threat to anyone."

The victim took a deep breath, and still obviously shaken, his shoulders relaxed a little.

Later, I found out more details from the lieutenant that arrived on the freeway from my department. He told me the Tempe lieutenant was transporting the 918 subject to a mental institution. The suspect sat through his cuffs in the back seat of the patrol car. To us in this profession, that meant the suspect was handcuffed behind his back but was flexible enough to bring his legs all the way up to his chest, subsequently bringing both cuffed hands in front of himself. The lieutenant pulled over to restrain the suspect again. When the lieutenant opened the patrol car, the guy managed to attack him. He then fought with the lieutenant and grabbed his handgun. He shot and killed this hero for no reason other than doing his job.

My supervisor looked at me. "So very sad. This man was due to retire soon. I just found out. So, officer, I'm going to tell you this. Never be afraid to ask for help, especially if you're not comfortable."

"Yes sir. I get it." I swallowed hard, his admonition sticking with me.

In the movies and on television, people get the impression that crime scenes clear up in an hour or so. Believe me, that was not the case with that situation. In my experience, no crime scene investigation ever cleans up fast. Between measurements, statements from witnesses, photographs, etc., it all takes time. I arrived on that scene around 3:30 p.m. and finally finished at 9:00 p.m., helping with whatever anyone needed from me.

When the medical examiner showed up, darkness already washed over the scene. While they moved the suspect's body onto their body bag, I noticed it turned a very dark color. Curious, I asked the investigator from the ME's office if it was normal for the deceased to turn that color?

He looked at me, a quizzical expression on his face. "You must be new."

"Yes, sir. A year-and-a-half." Up until then, I hadn't experienced this extremely dark coloring of a body.

The examiner went on to explain. "Because the scene needed to be processed, with the time it took and the high heat coming from the sun absorbing into the road's concrete, this is very typical."

I thanked him for the street lesson. By then, the fire department was on the scene with a ladder truck. They used their hose to pressure wash a black tarry substance off the freeway. The blood, at one time red, looked like black tar.

As I gathered up my traffic cones and

extinguished the road flares carefully placed at the scene, my thoughts turned to this lieutenant I never met. Here one minute and gone the next.

My own mortality came into question that night. I chose the profession of a police officer, and I had no regrets. I understood that I must continue to train and maintain officer safety the best I could.

No matter how good at my job I became, I could never be afraid to ask for help.

I climbed back in that piece of shit 1982 Chevrolet Malibu, a bit shaken, and took a deep breath. Then I picked up the mic and cleared. "4Frank11. Show me 10-8." Back in service.

"10-4, 4Frank11."

I drove into the night, waiting for the next call. No one asked about my emotions. No one suggested I take a break, or call it a day and go home. And no one expected me to do any less than finish my shift, including myself.

Later, I could take time to process the myriad of emotions—grief of losing a fellow officer, shock of watching a suspect die and turn a grotesque color, the weight of calming and comforting a victim, and realizing the job I chose could cost my life. A lot to process.

Still on duty, I pushed it all down and went back to work.

911 Hang up

South Phoenix—an area of town where police officers handle calls more frequently than in any other part of the city. Before too long on the force, I worked that area often.

On the job there for about a year-and-a-half, I worked homicides, aggravated assaults, rapes, and much more. We had our share of report calls over thefts, burglaries, and car accidents, plus alarm calls—and of course, 911 hang ups.

The 911 hang-up calls occurred when a person dialed 911 on their phone and subsequently, either hung up, or they disconnected—on purpose or not. Hence, the 911 hang up, where the dispatcher must send a police officer to the home, business, or area from where the call generated. With no additional information, we had to determine the origin and reason for the call and check the welfare of whoever placed it.

Sometimes, we found children playing on their parent's telephone, dialing 911. Other times, we caught a legitimate need for the police to handle a situation of an assault, domestic violence, or something menacing.

Working the night shift places strain on an officer's body. It's abnormal to work from nine at night until seven the next morning. Especially when the sun rises at 6:00 a.m., and you feel like Dracula needing to go back into your dark cave. Your eyes burn, and you just want to call it a day and go home.

On a bright, warm summer day in 1987, I worked in the South Mountain Precinct with the call sign of 4John25. From East 32nd Street to 48th Street, south to the mountain, I had a vast area to cover. Calls kept me constantly busy throughout my shift. The rising sun didn't bring radio silence with it.

The dispatcher cleared me. "4John25, I have no other units available. Please handle a 911 hang up at Central and Southern. 4John25, be advised you are rolling alone. There is no back up."

"4John25. 10-4."

It took a while to get to the address. On the far east side of the area, I had to travel west 48 streets to reach the location, but I finally arrived.

"4John25. Show me Code 6 at the location."

"10-4, 4John25. I'm still trying to get you a backup."

"OK. I'll advise. Thank you."

Our dispatchers truly cared for us out there on the street. They felt stress as much as we did and took it personally if anyone was injured. While some of the hang-up calls held no threat, some did. Answering any call alone presented a potential threat. I treasured dispatchers who cared.

The 911 hang up turned out to be at a nursing home. Sometimes, disgruntled residents placed calls, claiming mistreatment or that nurses neglected them. They often swore they suffered alone at death's door. Most of the time, they didn't hang up, but wanted someone outside of the nursing home to rescue them. Often, they only wanted to leave the facility, to escape somewhere less restrictive. On occasion, we saw true emergencies at the nursing homes.

Wondering which might be the case that morning, I walked through the main door. In the early morning, with nurses busy on the floor, I found myself in the kitchen area where the staff was preparing breakfast.

One employee looked up. "Hi, officer. Is there a problem?"

"I don't know. We received a 911 hang-up call from this location. Is everyone OK here?"

Mary, the staff coordinator, said, "Yes, we are fine back here in the kitchen. Is there a particular area the call came from?"

I shrugged. "Let me ask dispatch again." I keyed my tactical mic clip. "4John25. Do you have any further info on which area this call may have been generated from?"

"4John25. It looks like it came from the maintenance area."

Mary heard the dispatcher's reply and didn't hesitate. "Oh, officer, let me show you where the maintenance area is."

As we headed out of the kitchen, my sergeant showed up. "I heard you didn't have backup, so I came from the station."

"Thanks, Joe. I appreciate that." I meant it. Although everything seemed quiet and normal, no resident made a call from the maintenance area. This could be serious.

Mary led us down a long corridor. "When you get to the end of the hallway, turn right. Then make a left, and you'll see the maintenance office."

We thanked her and continued walking to the area while she returned to the kitchen.

Turning right around the corner, we stepped into a massive pool of blood seeping from a man lying on the floor. His right hand clutched a large knife.

No pulse.

Joe looked over at me. "Jesus."

We both cleared leather and launched a tactical search.

Moving forward, two more bodies. The stench of metal assaulted us. Tremendous amounts of blood covered the hallway.

High alert kicked in. We continued toward the maintenance area. Turning left into the office, we discovered three more bodies. Glassy eyes and immense loss of blood. No need to check pulses.

Blood coated our boots. My stomach turned queasy. Joe's face paled almost to white. No words needed. The gruesome scene held us by the throat.

No living person in the area. Murderer gone.

Joe contacted dispatch, advising numerous victims. He requested dispatch of homicide detectives to our location.

Dispatched acknowledged. "Their ETA is 20 minutes."

Joe and I secured the scene. Crime-scene tape encased the entire area. We couldn't allow a single person to enter before detectives arrived. Standing on guard, we had no idea what happened.

Spending numerous hours on the scene until a day shift unit relieved us, I asked myself, "How did this happen?"

The next day, I learned how the mass homicide played out.

Joe shared details he learned from the detectives. The first deceased body belonged to the suspect. Forensics showed his wound as self-inflicted. The other bodies in the maintenance office belonged to maintenance workers—three men and one woman.

The woman's family supplied additional information during the investigation. The suspect was distraught because the woman broke up with him earlier in the week. Apparently, he came to the maintenance office and approached her, threatening her with the knife. When her coworkers attempted to intervene, he killed them, along with the woman, stabbing them with the same knife he used on himself while leaving the area.

In that case, the threat ended with the subject's suicide. Haunting thoughts stuck with me. What if we ignored the call because someone hung up? What if he went berserk and attacked nurses, other employees, and even the residents? I shuddered at that thought.

That case solidified our need to always respond to any call. Going forward, I declared, "There is no bogus call. Don't ever take a 911 hang up as something meaningless or a prank."

Just ask me, I will tell you. They are not.

Don't Lie About Me

Every police officer knows that people do not tell the truth at times. Really? Yes, really.

In July 1988, I was working the day shift at the South Mountain Precinct in Phoenix, Arizona. Most calls at that time were report calls from the night before when people came home and found their cars or homes broken into. Hence, a report radio call was generated.

On a particular call, I received a 459 computer-generated call, more commonly referred to as a burglary call. The report was in my beat area, so I responded and was met by a portly man about 40 years of age. He was waiting for me in the street in front of his residence.

Right away, I got the "I was robbed" vernacular from this man, who identified himself as Rusty Knobb.

"Mr. Knobb, you were robbed at gunpoint?"

"No, I was not. They broke into my house."

"OK. You say they broke into your house. Do you know who they are?"

"No. Come on, officer. You know what I mean, don't you?"

"No, sir, I do not. I am here to investigate what happened, and that is why I have to be specific with these questions."

Mr. Knobb continued to walk around his home and show me where items the robbers took were previously located. The area where Mr. Knobb resided was very dilapidated, with run-down looking homes. Scattered wine bottles, liquor bottles, and beer cans and bottles dotted the street. Mr. Knobb's home appeared much the same as the others in the area. In my opinion, his story didn't jive. I found it hard to believe that over two thousand dollars' worth of property disappeared from that house, including multiple televisions and VCRs, along with some cash. Still, I took his information, dusted for fingerprints, and advised him that I was going to my patrol car to get his report number from our DR (departmental report) desk.

Entering from the passenger side of my patrol car, I logged back into my MDT and submitted the victim's name along with the location, time, and type of report number needed.

While waiting for the number from the DR desk, I always made it a habit to run my victims through the wants and warrants systems to check for any outstanding warrants.

That day, the sun bore down harshly, already in the high 90s in the Phoenix area. Sweat poured down my back and face, but I continued jotting notes on my report sheet.

Beep. Beep.

MDT alert, notifying me I had a message waiting. I needed to go. The guy was a dipshit. I planned to give him the report number and split. As I hit the next message on my computer, thinking I was getting the report number, I saw an unexpected message.

"HIGH RISK ALERT! Subject is a possible AIDS carrier."

Holy shit.

My heart stopped. Did he know? We still didn't know enough about the disease, but no one wanted close contact with a carrier. If he contracted it through needle use, that also indicated a risk of him being high, and I knew how quickly a situation could go south with a drug addict.

A voice behind me yelled, "What's that say about me having AIDS?"

Unbeknownst to me, the guy stood behind me. I jumped, angry at myself for letting him sneak up on me.

I pushed the screen away from his view. "No idea, sir."

"No, I want to see what it says."

"Sorry, sir. You have no right to see what this says or said. It is a departmental computer, utilized only for police personnel, not civilians such as yourself."

This went back and forth, his volume escalating. He grew more persistent.

I finally said, "The answer is still no. Here's your report number. If you have any more information regarding this crime, please refer to the report number and submit a follow up investigation form with the department."

"I'll call your supervisor," he shouted as I drove away.

Whatever asshole. Call him. You'll get The Squid.

The Squid was the sergeant on my squad—Sergeant Holly, the biggest jerk ever. He followed officers around, attempting to catch them doing something wrong. Anything, no matter how small. He pulled MDT messages to see anything other officers said to each other. He especially wanted to know what anyone said about him. The guy was just plain weird, if not paranoid.

I asked one of the veterans how they came up with the name Squid?

Officer Kaye told me, "Well, Jimbo, he has no backbone, like a squid."

I laughed. "Now it makes total sense." I agreed with the assessment.

Knobb did call my supervisor, the ever-famous Squid, who took his complaint with no reservation. You see, the Squid and I did not care for each other. I called him out several times, saying things such as, "Don't you have anything better to do than follow me around?"

The weird bastard just looked at me with the confused look he always portrayed. "What do you mean?"

He played this game repeatedly, and he played it well. Always wearing that lost look on his face, he was a conniving piece of whale shit that ruined some officers' careers. We didn't trust him ever to have our backs. More than likely, he held the knife used to stab one of us from behind.

The complaint went all the way up the chain. Even the chief of police was notified of Knobb's complaint. The upper command of the police department scrambled, trying to figure out who placed the information about Knobb in the computer database.

But for the time, it was the Squid's turn. He was chomping at the bit. One could tell just by looking at him. He took great joy at trying to make me feel uncomfortable with his comments and gestures, always wearing a shit-eating grin.

When the Squid interviewed Knobb, the dirtbag embellished what really transpired in our conversation at his place when I took the report. He went as far as saying I told him the MDT said he had AIDS, and the health department was the one reporting to the police department that he was a carrier. This statement was totally false. I never said anything to Knobb other than, "Here's your report number. Have a nice day."

Eventually, my turn with the Squid rolled around. He made some very disturbing allegations against me.

"Apparently, you went out of your way, telling Knobb he was an AIDS carrier. Saying, if it was you that they said those things about, you'd go to the newspaper and tell them how you were wrongly accused of being an AIDS carrier."

Unbelievable.

Maybe that's what Knobb wanted to do, but I never suggested it. We didn't discuss AIDS beyond him pressing me for what the screen showed, and I didn't admit it said anything about AIDS.

The Squid was persistent, trying to catch me in a lie. Every time he asked, and every memo he requested I write, I always told the same story. When you tell the truth, your story never changes. My story didn't change because I told how the entire incident went down.

After several months of back and forth, the conclusion of the Squids complaint was adjudicated—no evidence that I told Knobb what he claimed I said.

The Squid, being the Squid, tried to be my buddy after that. "I always knew there was nothing to this. I told the command staff this guy Knobb was lying."

Yeah right, Sure you did, asswipe. I didn't dignify him with an answer.

All during that time, I was processing with the Los Angeles PD, wondering if the complaint might work against me.

The Squid was always asking, "Hey, have you heard anything yet? When are you leaving for LA?"

My answer didn't sway. "No. Nothing yet." All the time, thinking he's the last guy I'll tell when I'm leaving. I felt certain he definitely had an ulterior motive—trying somehow to stick it to me before I left. Nothing about this man evoked my respect or trust.

My conclusion about the Squid? He'd never even be a pimple on any Los Angeles police officer's or supervisor's ass.

I worked with some great police officers in Phoenix and had some outstanding supervisors. Unfortunately, the Squid was not one of them. He was donkey shit and a very disturbed man.

If I learned anything from him, it was not ever to be that kind of person.

Black Canyon Freeway
Shooting

Phoenix PD Shot

Phoenix Walking Beat 2

Phoenix Walking
Beat 1

Steve Konegni and Jim
Calams with Jeff Cooper
at Gunsite

70

LAPD Graduation Picture

Mark Beadles (FTO) and Jim

The Los Angeles Police Academy—my First Hours, O Dark Thirty

I made it! June 18, 1990.

I was selected to enter the Los Angeles Police Academy. With over a year of waiting, taking tests, and physical and psychological exams, I finally made it.

A lifelong dream to become a Los Angeles Police Officer, seeing the culmination of all that work, left me surreal. At 0500 hours, I dressed in a sport coat and tie and joined 108 other recruits. Men and women alike. All races—African American, Hispanic, Asian, and Caucasian. None of that mattered.

Milling around in the academy gymnasium, we waited, some patiently, others full of anxiety.

The door popped open, and all the drill instructors (DI) from the academy entered the gym. "Get on the black line. Do it now!" The unison order left recruits scurrying.

The black line marked the entire perimeter of the basketball court. One thing I learned from already being through a police academy in Phoenix, Arizona six years earlier was to keep my mouth shut, look forward, and do what you're told. Solid on my spot at the black line, I waited at attention for the next order.

"Stand at attention!"

Obvious to me, some of those folks selected to enter the academy had no clue what to expect. Several talked back to the DIs.

My mind raced. *I can't believe these idiots are questioning these guys. What are they? Stupid? Oh, my gosh they must be stupid.* I watched from across the gym as some recruits were doing pushups with DIs in their faces.

"You call that a push up? My grandmother can do better," one instructor said with a stern voice.

One of the recruits laughed. Another snickered.

"Who thinks this is funny?" The DI blurted. "Is it you?"

He singled out a recruit. "Get down and start doing pushups 'til I tell you to stop. You understand me?"

"Yeah."

"Yeah? Are you kidding me? You come with me." The DI escorted him from the gym.

From experience, I knew that recruit was about to have his first come to Jesus meeting.

I kept my mouth shut, but I couldn't stop the flow of amazement. *This is craziness. How the hell did some of these people get selected?* I stood at attention on the black line near a rear door leading to a sidewalk. The door was closed, but in a crazy moment, it squeaked open. Knowing better, I didn't turn around.

This young woman came to the line and pushed me to the side. "Let me in, please."

I scooted over a bit, keeping eyes forward and never breaking attention or responding to her.

Three DIs apparently saw the door open. They ran toward me.

Ohhh shit. I shouldn't have moved.

All three came up to the woman, and one addressed her. "Thank you so much for coming." The sarcasm dripped from his voice. "Why are you late?"

"Sorry. I was stuck in traffic." She answered

with a nonchalant tone, as if arriving late didn't matter much.

"Did you not come to family night last week? What time were you supposed to be here? What were you supposed to wear?"

"No, I had to work."

"Where do you think you are? In Hollywood?" The DI didn't let up.

At family night, which happened one week prior to the start of the academy, they told us to dress in a sport coat and tie for the men. The women were to wear a conservative blouse and pants. I glanced at the woman with my peripheral vision. She showed up in a mini skirt and high-heeled shoes. Her top looked like it might split at the seams.

The DI fumed. "You're going to the bathroom and take off that war paint on your face, the short skirt, top, and hooker shoes. We will bring you a change of clothes."

The recruit retreated toward the restroom like a chastised child.

By that time, I wanted to laugh. The situation wasn't funny, yet this woman getting busted made me want to crack up. She should have known better. A female cop only dressed like a hooker if she went undercover and needed to play that role.

A male DI brought in sweatpants, a top, and some used tennis shoes. He gave the items to a female DI. Without a word, she took the clothes and headed toward the restroom.

The whole time, one of the DIs took a position right next to me, staring me in the face. It took all I had not to crack a smile or move, but I didn't. I remained focused and followed every command shouted that morning.

They shuffled us around from room to room, where we received our leather gear, recruit uniforms, physical training sweat gear, and t-shirts. At our last stop, the firearms unit, they issued our duty weapons.

The sergeant from the firearms unit took extra effort to keep his instructions unmistakable. "Do not touch the handgun! Put the box with your handgun in your warbag and do not touch it until told to."

With those two obvious do not's, I stowed my handgun in my warbag.

Well, guess what? Two people apparently had a hearing problem. While admiring their handguns, they were introduced to the hill behind the firearms unit.

A DI escorted the two recruits to the hill that inclines at least 70 degrees. The DI relaxed at the bottom, running the two up the hill and down several times. We all knew that hill, and let me say, it's a bitch running it in PT gear. Imagine how much more so doing it in a suit and tie, wearing dress shoes.

How the hell did these guys get picked to be here? Again, I couldn't shake my astonishment.

The main DI for our class, Officer Todd Rhiengold, was a veteran of the department with lots of hash marks on his sleeve. Todd, all business, outshined most recruits with his physique and physical abilities. Standing 6' 6", not a pound of fat existed on this guy.

Although the methods that day seemed harsh to some, Todd's commanding presence overpowered any foolishness. He spoke the truth every recruit in our class needed to hear. "If you can't cut it here, you sure as hell won't cut it in the mean streets of Los Angeles."

The room fell silent as his voice boomed against the walls and bounced back. "I repeat. I will not graduate anyone here that may cause harm to the many brave men and women in the

Los Angeles Police Department. Do you understand me?"

"Yes, Sir," every recruit yelled back in unison.

"Let me know now if you don't want to be here. You can go back to bagging groceries at Vons. I'll make that happen for you. Are we clear?"

The recruits responded louder than before. "Yes, Sir!"

I thought surely, we'd been there for hours by then. Only two hours into the day, I said to myself, "Boy, this is going to be a long day. These assholes need to get it together." The recruits with nonchalant attitudes grated on my nerves.

Finally, the DI introduced us to a classroom for our book instruction. Placed in alphabetical order for our seat assignments, I sat near the front. A last name starting with the letter C, I had no issue with being at the front of the class.

In the classroom, I met a young recruit by the name of Hubert Nino. He preferred to go by Nino. He was telling another recruit how hard he worked to get to the academy while the listener acted like he couldn't care less.

I went up to Nino and introduced myself. "Hey, brother, I'm Jim Calams." Extending my hand, Nino grasped it firmly.

"Nice to meet you."

As we put our things together at our desks, Nino told me how his mother and father immigrated to the United States years earlier. His parents worked very hard to provide for their family and instilled that motivation and dedication in their children. Nino spoke of how people are discriminated against at times, admitting his parents endured it. But they stayed the course, working hard and providing for their family.

In our brief conversation, I mentioned to Nino how my grandparents immigrated from Greece. They knew discrimination too, but worked hard to provide for their children. "I get it, Nino. Welcome. I look forward to more talks. You have something to be very proud of as a Los Angeles police recruit.

"Me too, Jim."

I looked forward to encouraging this young man who understood working hard, and I expected him to become a fine officer. He had the drive to make it.

When we finally got a break, I met another man. To this day, he remains my best friend from Los Angeles.

He approached me. "Hey, bud, my name is James. What's yours?"

"Hey, I'm Jim Calams."

"What did you do before coming here?"

"I was a Phoenix police officer."

"Cool, brother. James Edwards at your service."

We shook hands, and he smiled at me. "Hey, Phoenix. We better get back in the classroom. We don't want to be late."

Edwards called me Phoenix throughout our entire six months at the academy. Separated by miles and time, he's a true friend who would do anything for me or my family. And in return, he knows I'd get my gear at a moment's notice and head his way for him and his family.

Love you, brother, always and forever. Stay safe.

Just Beat It

During the summer of 1993, I worked at the West Los Angeles Division assigned to unit 8X98 mid-pm watch. On a hot August night, at 2345 hours, I received a computer MDT message from the watch commander, Sgt-2 Bill Del Atorre. He wanted my partner and me to come to the West LA station due to the severity of a call he needed us to handle.

Sgt. Del Atorre, a veteran of the LAPD, owned my utmost respect. He stood 6′ 1″ with 200 pounds of solid muscle—the epitome of working out and staying in shape. By computer, I responded, *no problem, Bill.* I would do anything for Del Atorre—a man who always showed leadership not only to me, but to all police officers who had the honor of working for him.

Arriving at the station, we went directly to

the watch commander's office and met up with Sgt. Del Atorre. A woman who identified herself as Judy Smart waited in the office with him. Ms. Smart was a field investigator for the Department of Children and Family Services.

After the introduction, Del A Torre leaned forward. "I'm sorry to do this to you, but you were the only clear unit in the division. Due to the severity of the allegation that Ms. Smart will tell you about here shortly, I'm going to need you both to handle this situation. She'll explain what needs to be done tonight."

My curiosity aroused, I leaned forward.

Del Atorre turned the conversation over to Ms. Smart.

"Guys, I'm going to need you to follow me to a location where the father at this residence in Brentwood has contacted our department. He made a disturbing allegation of sexual abuse on several occasions against his son Ryan."

Great. A molestation case. My curiosity waned. "Can't dayshift take the report?"

"No." Ms. Smart scooted forward in her chair. "The alleged perpetrator named in this case is a well-known, worldwide celebrity."

My partner, Officer Smith, leaned back in

his chair. "Who might that be?"

Smart pursed her lips. "Michael Jackson."

"You mean 'Beat It' Michael Jackson?" Smith straightened up.

"The one and only." Smart rubbed her forehead. "Officers, we need to get out to the home and get this documented by the police department ASAP."

Uncertain what to think, we all went to our vehicles. I followed Smart.

As we approached the Brentwood area, I couldn't help but marvel. Back in 1993, the tiniest house in that neighborhood had a value of over one million dollars. On a police officer's salary, I never dared dreamed of living in such an upscale and affluent area.

We arrived at the residence, a beautiful home from the outside. Definitely a family with big bucks. After knocking on the door, the owner, Ryan's father, welcomed us.

"Hello, everyone. I'm Herschel. Please come in." We exchanged handshakes as if we stood in the grandeur of wealth every day.

"Please come back here." Hershel led us all into the living room. "Everyone, this is my son, Ryan. Please sit down. Everybody."

Looking at the boy, the house lost its luster. Nothing mattered but hearing the child.

Smart started the conversation with the father. "I have briefed the officers, and we are here to listen to Ryan, ask him questions, and document them on a police report."

"Great. Let's get started." Hershel didn't hesitate.

Smart looked at Smith and me. "I want to go into the den and interview Ryan, but I need only one of you in there with me. Which one will it be?"

"Let's flip a coin," Smith said. "Call it, Jimbo."

"Heads!"

"Heads it is. What do you want to do?"

"I'll take the report, Smith. No big deal."

Ryan, Smart, and I entered the den area, partitioned off by white wooden folding doors. A luxurious, soft leather dark-brown couch along with a recliner invited us inside. Pictures decorated the walls, adding a pleasant background to the wood floor throughout the den. I avoided the recliner, figuring it might be a bit too comfortable in the middle of the night. Ryan's dog sidled up next to him, alert but relaxed.

Smart got right to business. "OK, let's get started." She faced the boy. "Ryan, do you know the difference between right and wrong?"

"Yes, I do." Ryan seemed confident.

"I want you to tell me in your own words what's been going on with you and Michael Jackson. Are you OK talking about this?"

No reluctance, his voice steady. "Yes."

Ryan started by saying he met Jackson initially through his stepdad. He said that his mother, who owned a rental car company, met Jackson when one of his limousines broke down near her corporate offices. Both the mom and stepdad conducted their business in that office.

Ryan said the stepdad and mom both kept in contact with Jackson by phone after that, saying how much their son "just loves you."

The stepdad and mom told Jackson, "He even dresses like you at times. His room at our home has numerous posters and Jackson memorabilia all over it."

The child relayed that his mom showed Jackson pictures of him, and Jackson became very interested, wanting to meet him. He invited the mother and Ryan to visit his home in Santa Barbara, with overnight stays at Neverland.

Jackson had Ryan and his mother visit Neverland in early February 1992. Ryan said he had a blast playing unlimited video games in the game room and arcade. During that first visit in February 1992, he stayed overnight with his mother occupying the guest quarters, which was far away from the main building where Ryan slept.

He said, "It was pretty far away, officer, where mom was."

Ryan described a very large circular bed inside the main bedroom. He told us that Jackson had several other young males at the ranch, including Hollywood child stars. Ryan said that Jackson would lounge on the center of the large circular bed and select a young boy randomly. The two then went into another room.

"It was a bathroom, officer." He shifted in his chair, his voice becoming shaky as he started discussing that part of his story.

I reassured the boy. "It's OK, Ryan. Go ahead." He looked at the floor, so I comforted him. "I understand. Take your time."

Ryan drew in a quick breath, then continued. "He selected me on that first night after a few hours. Jackson crawled up beside me and cuddled next to me in the bed while others watched. Then Jackson kissed me on the cheek, extended his hand, and led me to the other room, which was a large bathroom."

I wasn't sure I wanted to hear more, but I leaned forward in my chair, intent on what this kid had to say.

"Once the door closed, Jackson continued to kiss me on the face, neck, mouth, and ears. He used his tongue the entire time to penetrate my mouth and ears."

Trying not to vomit at the allegations, I swallowed hard.

Ryan continued with his story as Smart and I listened and took notes. Throughout the year of 1992, he allegedly made several trips to Jackson's residence with his mother—always the same scenario. He stayed with Jackson, and his mom stayed in the far away guest quarters.

Ryan said "their love" grew into a fondness toward each other. When Jackson invited Ryan to France in 1993, Mom tagged along. Ryan said he spent over half a month in France with

Jackson, touring the cities during the day and sleeping with him at night. His mom stayed in a separate room for the entire trip.

Ryan told me their relationship became very sexual. He said Jackson would present his penis and start rubbing it aggressively, telling Ryan the whole time how he cared for him.

Then Ryan told me something very odd. "Officer, he squirted 'duck juice' all over me."

"Ryan, duck juice? What are you talking about?" A streetwise cop, I hadn't heard that phrase.

"Ya know, officer. He masturbated on me."

"Where Ryan?"

"On my body."

"Did Jackson call it duck juice?"

"Yes, sir, he did."

I jotted down a note. "OK, Ryan, continue." I again assured him everything was going to be OK.

As Ryan relived the experiences, he tugged at his shirt, biting his lip. The dog moved closer and Ryan petted him. It appeared the animal was a therapy dog. It calmed him down as the boy continued rubbing his fur.

I took a breath. "What's your dog's name,

Ryan?"

"Wolfy. He's my best friend."

"Very nice, Ryan. I have a dog too, at my house. Dogs are great."

We all sat in silence for a few minutes, allowing Ryan time to regroup before we continued.

Suddenly, *BRAAAACK. FRRRT.* A beat. *PFFT.*

Ryan's eyes flew wide. "Officer, what was that?"

"Well, Ryan, it wasn't Wolfy."

"I'm sorry, I have gas." Smart's face looked like she spent the last 24 hours in the sun. She put her hand over her mouth and cringed.

Oh my gosh! It stunk so bad!

What a nasty lady. Why would you not excuse yourself for a few minutes if you felt the urge to blow farts our way? The thoughts flowed freely as I refrained from voicing them.

In the seriousness of the moment, no one laughed. Wishing for an open window, we took another moment to regain our composure and let the air clear of the stench.

Then I continued with questions. "Ryan, explain to me what else happened with your relationship that was sexual in nature."

Ryan paused, looking uncomfortable. "Well, officer, during the stay in France, it was pretty much every day, Michael played with me."

"Explain play, Ryan."

"He would put his hand in my pajama pants, rubbing my penis very hard, which would make me kinda pee."

By then, I worked hard to conceal the emotions rising in me. I couldn't let them show for fear of shutting down the kid. Ryan stated they had a ritual where Jackson and he bathed together in the hotel bathtub during their time in France.

"He would say to me, 'I love you, sweet boy.' I believed him." Ryan fought back tears as Wolfy came closer, comforting his young charge.

"It's OK, Ryan. I am here to help you get through this." Everything in me fought to stay calm. "I know it's very traumatic to relive this, but we are here to help you."

"I know you are, officer." Ryan gasped a bit and cleared his throat as his eyes glistened.

"What happened in the bathtub, Ryan?"

"Michael would rub my penis a lot. He kept kissing me, saying, 'Rub me, sweet boy. Don't stop. I want you to watch my duck juice come out.' Michael would reach under the water and grab my penis and put it in his mouth. He sucked on it until I peed in his mouth. He would be so happy when it happened, saying, 'Oh, this duck juice is so sweet my pretty boy.'" Ryan swiped at a couple tears that managed to escape.

Needless to say, while I took notes and listened to Ryan, thoughts ran rampant. This guy Jackson was a sick bastard. But I wondered, why is this kid allowing it to happen to him?

"Ryan, I need you to answer two questions for me. OK?"

"Yes, sir."

"Where was your mother the whole time this was going on? And was this the only time when you and Michael were together doing this—the half month you were together in France?"

"Mom had her own room. She didn't sleep with me. Michael and I slept together in the room. And no, it happened at another place."

"Where, Ryan?"

He swallowed. "It was at my dad's house, where I stay sometimes."

"Explain about what happened at your dad's place, Ryan."

"Michael came to visit me one time, and he slept overnight in my room."

"Your dad's house?"

"Yes, sir, in my room. He slept on the pullout."

"Pullout. What is that?"

"My half-stepbrother, Sammy, and I sleep in the same room. We have stackable bunk beds, and there is a pullout section on the bottom bunk area. If we have somebody who stays the night, friends or whatever, we have the extra bed for a sleepover."

I nodded. "OK. When did he visit, Ryan?"

"Oh, it was earlier this year. Springtime, I think."

I noted that Ryan referred to spring 1993. "Ryan, what happened in the bedroom the night Michael stayed over at your dad's house here?"

"We waited for Sammy to fall asleep. Michael cuddled next to me in my bunk. He kissed me, played with my penis. He wanted me to play with him."

"Did you?"

"Yes, I did." Ryan's voice dropped almost to a whisper as he responded. This went on for quite some time with Jackson in Ryan's bunk bed. "After Michael finished, we went to sleep."

"When you say finished, what do you mean, Ryan?" I didn't want to leave anything to chance and lose this creep because I made an assumption about anything.

"Michael would say, 'Sweet boy, oh the duck juice. Let's sleep now my sweet boy.'"

It was apparent by Ryan's response to that question that Jackson climaxed sexually and then wanted to sleep.

"Is there anything else you can think of, Ryan, that you would like to tell me?" I prayed Jackson didn't go farther with this kid. I might have lost it if that was the case.

Ryan brightened. "Only that Michael is very kind. He buys me gifts. We go to toy stores, and he tells me to pick out whatever I want. He pays for everything."

"Anything else, Ryan, that you would like to tell Miss Smart and myself?"

Sadness covered the child's face. "Well, my

dad and my mom argue a lot."

"What do you mean, Ryan?"

"Dad gets mad when Mom lets me stay with Michael. He tells her I am spending too much time there. My dad is very concerned. I know Dad has an attorney and discussed a settlement."

"What do you mean about a settlement, Ryan?"

He shrugged. "I don't know, officer. You'll have to ask my dad."

"Anything else you can tell me, Ryan?"

"No. That's all I can remember."

"Thank you, Ryan, for trusting me with this whole situation and reliving what happened. I am going to talk to your dad now for a bit."

"Thank you, officer. You are very kind, and it was nice talking to you and Miss Smart." Ryan seemed calmer, but Wolfy stuck with him as he left the room.

I took a moment to collect my thoughts, to digest all this kid told us. Then, Dad's turn. We brought him into the den.

"Sir, I had no idea that Jackson stayed here at your home."

"Yes, officer. A few times. I knew there

were shenanigans going on."

"Please explain to me what you mean by shenanigans?"

"Well, the second time that I knew he was coming over here to spend the night, I hid microphones in Ryan's room."

"Microphones? Please explain, sir."

"Baby monitors. I hid two of them in the room."

"And what, if anything, did you hear?"

"Well, I heard a lot of laughing, giggling."

"Who was doing all that?"

"I heard Ryan, Sammy, and of course, Jackson."

"Anything else, sir?"

"Yes, I heard a lot of moaning. I could hear Ryan and Michael making a lot of moaning noises."

When the dad made that statement, I clenched my teeth for a minute before asking a question that burned hot in me. "Sir, this is your home, right?"

"Yes, it is officer."

I almost lost it at that point. "But why would you not rush right into Ryan's room and see what was occurring?"

"I was scared. Jackson brought his bodyguard with him. This guy was big and had muscles and was mean looking. I was afraid to go past him."

In my wildest imagination, I couldn't envision any man keeping me from my child in that scenario. I pushed that thought down.

"What's this about a settlement Ryan mentioned to me?"

"Yeah, I contacted an attorney. I told him what was going on with my son. My attorney contacted Michael's attorney."

"OK. Well, how did that play out?"

"My attorney said Michael's attorney said we could 'Go to hell' and that they would pay us nothing."

"So let me recap this with you." I looked down at my notes, then back at the dad. "You contacted your attorney. You told your attorney about what was happening sexually with your son and Jackson. Now you are requesting a settlement—a cash settlement. Am I correct with this?"

The dad grew rigid, sweat popping out on his brow. "Yeah, you're correct, but it sounds kinda mean the way you put it to me in that regard."

I didn't like this father much. "Anything else, sir?"

"No, that's it."

Not only was my stomach nauseous from listening to what Ryan alleged Jackson did, but now the dad was holding up his kid to the highest bidder and pissed they told him and his attorney to take a hike. If they had paid, would we be sitting in his home?

Only in Los Angeles.

I finished my notes, thinking to myself. *Who'd ever think? Fast forward a kid from the Midwest, several years later as a Los Angeles Police Officer, that I would be taking a report involving Michael Jackson as an alleged suspect. I would never imagine this–never.*

We left the home and headed back to the station to write the report. Closing in on 4:30 a.m. as I finished the report, I went to the watch commander in the West LA station for his review. He had to sign off on it.

He read the report and signed it. "Calams take this to the Sex Assaults desk at Parker Center. They will get a DR number. Don't talk to anybody about this. Seal it in this envelope.

Go now. They're waiting for it."

At 6:00 a.m., I was off to Parker Center—drained. I just finished listening to some sick shit for hours. A dad with his own agenda, trying to get money from the Jackson camp. I arrived at the "Glasshouse" Parker Center, went up to the Sexual Assaults office, and handed over the sealed manila envelope that contained my report.

A very nice secretary took it, saying, "We have been waiting for this. Thank you."

Finally, time to go home.

My lovely wife greeted me. "How was your night? Were you busy? Anything new?"

Under orders not to talk about the case, I choked down all the gunk raging inside me. "No, not really. I'm just exhausted."

I crashed into bed, hoping to get some sleep.

Waking at 3:30 p.m., I trudged downstairs.

My wife had the television on. She stared straight at me. "What in the Lord's name did you do last night?"

"Say what?"

"Your name is all over the TV, connected to Michael Jackson."

"Oh, yeah." I shrugged. "I was told not to

talk about it. Obviously, somebody released it to the news."

She wisely asked no more about it. Before I left for work, though, I explained to her what transpired the previous night.

I left for the mid-pm watch at West LA station. It looked the same as when I left. As I arrived and walked through the front door, George Laskey greeted me. George was a 25-year veteran of the LAPD, assigned to permanent desk duty. Super lazy with a tendency to piss off the public, they stuck him at the front desk to keep an eye on him. Despite all that, George was a great guy. He'd give you the shirt off his back.

He shouted across the room, "Jimbo! Hey, Mr. Hollywood."

My checks grew hot. "What the hell is that all about, George?"

"You're the talk of the town." He grinned. "Check your mailbox. You'll see. These people have been calling here all day. They're pissing me off. Shit, I hung up on some of them, and I am still hanging up on them." He laughed.

George didn't let anything get to him, and his humor spread. We both laughed about the craziness.

I went to my mailbox. There must have been over 50 pink message slips to contact various newspapers, magazines, and other publications that wanted to interview me.

"Don't even think about contacting them." I looked up to see the station captain watching me review the slips. "That will get you fired."

"No worries. I will not contact anyone. They told me last night not to say a word. Hell, I didn't even tell my wife last night, and now I'm in the dog house with her."

The captain burst out laughing. "Well, Calams, flowers may work."

"Yes, sir, that's my plan."

The phone calls continued throughout the week when the scandal hit all the papers. The story was all over the news channels. Like a wildfire, it spread everywhere—talk of the town.

I avoided listening whenever possible, hoping the gossip died down. In December 1993, I received a subpoena for a deposition. When I arrived at the attorney's office, a pleasant woman greeted and offered me a coffee. She had me take a seat in the waiting room. For at least two hours, I waited with no one appearing or calling me back to an inner office. Approaching the lunch hour, an actual attorney came out to meet me. Finally.

"Hey, why don't you go to lunch and come back, let's say around 1:30 p.m.?"

Anything felt better than the endless waiting, and my stomach agreed. "OK, see you then."

I went to lunch at my favorite "Pop spot" as we called it on patrol. Song Hay—the best Chinese in the city.

Ye knew me well and greeted me that day. "Oh, Officer Jim, you look so different."

"Yeah, I get dressed up once in a while, Ye." We both chuckled.

After enjoying my favorite Kung Pao Chicken lunch, I went back to the attorney's office only to sit yet another few hours. I flipped through magazines, checked the time, and got a drink of water. Checked the time again. Repeated.

At 3:20 p.m., the same attorney came out. "You're released, officer."

I scrunched my brows. "Are you going to re-subpoena me for a different time?"

"No. We are done."

"OK." Dumbfounded, I left. Amidst the confusion, anger simmered. As usual, I pushed it down, willing to process it all later. I got into my white Toyota pickup and headed north on the 405 Freeway. From habit, I turned on the radio.

Listening to a local Los Angeles station for traffic conditions, I learned more than the attorney told me. The announcer made his opinion obvious with his word choice.

"A payoff. Michael Jackson's accuser refused to cooperate with the authorities. What money will do to someone." He opened phone lines for the public to voice their opinion.

People phoned in, offering up some crazy conversation about all the mess. Some women called in, crying on the phone. The announcer loved every minute of the drama, playing it up to get more people calling, mounting the drama, and getting feedback from both sides. Some supported Jackson, while others seethed.

I turned the damn radio off. Unbelievable. "What a bunch of shit." In the safety of my truck, I could shout when necessary. At that moment, I wanted nothing more than to scream so loud they'd hear me all the way back in Chicago.

I calmed myself before arriving at home, where my sweet and lovely wife welcomed me.

"Did you hear?" I asked.

"Yup, I heard, sweetheart. I heard."

I lounged in my home, relaxing on my couch that afternoon, trying not to think about the turn of events and not wanting to hear another word about the case. But my mind couldn't shrug off the memories of Ryan's words in that big, fancy house and the reality of a celebrity's money and power.

My wife looked at me. "What are you thinking about?"

I responded, "Only in Los Angeles, sweetie. Only in Los Angeles."

1994 Northridge Earthquake

People who live in California grow accustomed to small earthquakes. Although the state experiences an estimated 10,000 per year, most register so small on the Richter scale, they go unnoticed. [1]

On January 17, 1994, we noticed.

This day remains etched in my mind, an unforgettable moment embedded there forever. The Northridge Earthquake.

At approximately 4:31 a.m., registering a severe 6.7, the earthquake centered in Northridge, striking Southern California with earth-shattering aftershocks that far outweighed the physical aftermath. With a revised death toll of 72 and thousands injured, the damage amounted to $20 billion and over

---

[1] (Writer 2020)

$40 billion in economic loss. Experts still consider it the costliest earthquake disaster in U.S. history. [2]

At home that early morning, asleep with my wife, our home shook violently. No warning. Not the way anyone wants to wake up, either. My body hit the floor—my wife also thrown from our bed. For a startled moment, my mind grasped for an explanation. Within seconds, she and I regained our composures, grabbed our children, and ran to the front yard.

During those moments, the earth continued to shake harshly. Our children clung to us, crying, shaking. Terror and confusion filled their little eyes. My wife and I did our best to put on a brave front for them, but as the earth vibrated below our feet, the same fear lurked within us. Every time we thought the earthquake stopped, an aftershock rolled through the ground and traveled up to our brains, leaving us afraid to move, yet wondering if we should escape with our kids.

Less than a minute later, although it felt like an hour, the ground finally grew still. We

---

[2] (California Department of Conservation 2007)

checked for structural damage within our home, and by the grace of God, all appeared ok.

Fast forward to early morning. My landline telephone rang.

I looked at my wife. "Wow! We have phone service?"

Neither of us thought to check the phone, assuming it didn't work after the earthquake. I answered it.

Dave Rossi, my watch commander from the West Los Angeles station, skipped any pleasantries. "Calams get into work ASAP! If you can't get out, the Palmdale Sheriff station's helicopter will fly you and other officers in the area down to Ramirez Street. We'll pick you up from there."

The Palmdale/Lancaster neighborhood had quite a few police officers living in my area of LA county. Ramirez Street houses the LAPD air unit station and police helicopters.

Rather than fly out, I decided to try driving. I left home at 9 a.m., thinking it wouldn't take much longer than usual to get there.

The 14 Freeway collapsed at the 5 Freeway intersection where I needed to go south on the 5 Freeway. Flipping a U-turn and heading down the shoulder of the 14, the California Highway Patrol stopped me. They ultimately escorted me out of the area, where I was able to get to the 405 Freeway and make my way to the west LA station.

"Oh my God. What a cluster fuck this is!" I yelled in my car. Despite the earliness of the day, the sky smothered the area with darkness—as dark as nighttime with no street lights on, people driving, and acting crazy.

Almost two-and-a-half hours later, I reached the station. Meeting with a cadre of officers, we waited impatiently for our assignments.

"Calams and Godinez, you have the ramp and the top of the bridge at Mulholland Drive at the 405. Get a black and white and get out there ASAP," explained Rossi.

The choice for my partner, Adolf Godinez, pleased me. A great guy, we worked together before on the mid pm shift at West LA.

Godinez shook his head. "You believe this shit, Jimbo?"

"I know, brother. It took me forever to get here."

As we drove through the streets, I entered a

hyper-vigilant state, the hair on my arms prickling. Erie. The darkness closed in around our squad car. Only our headlights pierced the black. Little to no movement on the street.

My mind retraced all the apocalyptic movies I ever watched. The gloom and sense of despair pressed in, leaving my chest feeling heavy. Surely the end of the world was coming. At least it seemed that way as we drove in silence. I sensed Godinez felt it as deeply as I did.

I swallowed hard, constantly checking my rearview mirrors, half expecting a zombie-like creature to pop out from the shadows. My rabbit-paced heart didn't help the situation. I took deep breaths, calming myself, yet remained at full alert.

After what seemed like hours, in reality not long at all, we arrived at our assigned location and blocked the area. No person or vehicle could enter. The bridge sustained major damage and had the possibility of total collapse. Our assignment—protect unsuspecting people from being on the bridge if it went down.

We took our position, and the occasional driver came by, wanting to pass. We turned them away. Some were nice about it, understanding and thankful. Others—complete assholes.

The whole time, the RTO (dispatcher) kept putting out a broadcast for a missing elderly man. He had been missing for over eight hours. We listened as the RTO relayed that Mr. B was an 85-year-old man, diagnosed with Alzheimer's. He was driving a brown Lincoln Town Car.

Mrs. B, the wife, told our watch commander that her husband left their home at 4 p.m. to check on a business he owned. She hadn't seen him since.

We heard from the watch commander. The wife was hysterical, calling the station numerous times. "She kept begging us, 'Find him please! Find him. I love him so much.' Poor woman. She's beside herself."

As the repeated bulletin kept coming over the radio, Godinez and I looked at each other throughout the night. After multiple times of hearing it, we both said what we'd been thinking. "I suspect this guy is no longer amongst the living."

Around midnight, Sergeant Mitch stopped

by our location. "How are you doing?"

"We're good."

We chatted a moment, then he asked, "Hey, you guys been hearing about the missing elderly man?"

"Yeah. It's a damn shame, Sarge. Not looking good for him." Both Godinez and I felt bad and hated saying the words. As cops, we tended to look at life realistically more than with hope. Anyone missing that long—not a good sign. As much as we wanted to hope, we knew the statistics.

As Mitch and Godinez continued chatting, my mind drifted back to the days when I attended the Police Academy.

My drill instructor, Todd Rheingold, repeatedly told us in our class, "One never quits, one never gives up. You never quit. Never!"

I didn't want to quit on the old man, but facts don't lie. We lived reality, and it screamed the odds against an 85-year-old man surviving this catastrophe.

Sergeant Mitch's voice pulled me back. He wanted to give us a lunch break. "I heard there was a place open in the West Valley area. Go take a break, get some food."

I looked at Mitch. "Hey, we're going to look for this guy."

Godinez looked at me, his eyes wide. "Are you kidding, Jimbo?"

"No buddy. Let's go find this guy."

Sergeant Mitch shook his head and smiled. "If you find him, I will write you the best commendation. Not only that, I'll buy you both a steak dinner."

"Deal, Sarge." We all knew he might be dead, but better for his wife to know than wonder. Someone needed to locate Mr. B. "Let's roll, Adolf."

As we winded through the dark streets, we headed down the hill into the valley area of Los Angeles—the West Valley area, to be specific.

Around 20 minutes went by as we searched the area for this brown Lincoln Town Car.

Suddenly Godinez said, "Hey, let's go down Ventura Blvd. It's a main drag. Maybe the guy is around there."

"Good idea."

We started driving down Ventura Blvd. Not quite the same ghost town as earlier, many cars traveled on the street, along with some foot traffic from local residents.

As Godinez drove down Ventura, I spotted a LA Sheriff's deputy car talking to another person. The deputies ultimately drove off.

Even with the area in darkness, I thought, "Shit, that looks like a Lincoln chatting with the deputy." Could it be our guy?

"Adolf, turn around back where the deputy was."

"Why?"

"I think we found our missing man, brother."

"Bull shit. Come on. A deputy just stopped there. It can't be him."

I had a gut feeling. "No, turn this car around."

Regardless of his doubts, my partner complied.

We pulled up behind the brown Lincoln, and I activated the red lights. Adolf sounded the horn. About to pull away from the curb, the Lincoln stopped.

I keyed my mic and cleared the dispatcher. "Verifying California license number for missing elderly man."

The dispatcher's voice returned, filled with

excitement. "Unit 802, that is correct. Do you have the vehicle?"

"Yes ma'am. Show us code 6 with that vehicle and notify the watch commander. We're stepping out for inspection."

"Roger."

Godinez and I flanked the vehicle, contacting the driver. The elderly driver appeared alive and well, although mystified.

"Mr. B, are you OK?"

"Yes sir, I am." Tears welled up in his clouded eyes. "But I'm lost."

My heart wanted to wrap my arms around the old man, but I refrained. "It's OK, sir. My partner and I are going to get you home. Come with me in my car, and my friend, Adolf, will drive yours."

A single tear rolled down his wrinkled cheek. "OK, sir, thank you. I am sure my wife is worried."

I choked back a lump. "Yes, she is."

As we left the area, I cleared on the radio. "Unit 802. Show us en route to Mr. B's residence. Advise his wife. He is alive and well and can't wait to see her."

"802, roger." Over the radio, I detected

incredulous relief in the dispatcher's tone.

The watch commander cleared me over the radio to switch to our talk Channel 2. I switched.

Rossi came on. "I just can't believe that guy is OK. Are you sure?"

"Yes, sir. He's fine. A bit tired, but he will be fine." I shared his surprise, still barely believing we found him alive.

"Great work by both of you. His wife is ecstatic. I just hung up the phone with her."

"Roger that, sir."

As Godinez and I approached the home of Mr. and Mrs. B, she came running out of the house. Heck, I almost hit her with the black and white.

She was crying and smiling at the same time. "Oh, you're home. You're home. I've missed you so much." She kept repeating the words while they hugged and kissed repeatedly.

After several minutes, we accompanied the couple into their home. Mrs. B hugged and kissed Godinez and me several times, thanking us. "Let me get you some beer. You want some beer?"

Not a question of want. We were still on

duty. "No ma'am. We are good, thank you."

We so often saw tragedy, and that night could have ended so differently. My heart burst with pride for following my instincts and joy over the reunion. Such a great experience in my career as a Los Angeles police officer to see such amazing people have a happy ending. They loved each other immensely. Watching the two of them together, we had no doubt about that.

As we continued our meeting with the couple, getting further information for our report, the two of them showed us their forearms. Etched there crudely, numbers made my skin prickle. These two fine people survived the Auschwitz death camps during WWII.

The woman stroked her husband's forearm. "Do you know what this is, officers?"

"Yes ma'am, we sure do," we replied simultaneously.

I added, "We are so happy you both are reunited again."

We said our goodbyes, but the kisses and hugs continued, which was fine with us. Their gratitude and show of affection left us smiling, happy to reunite someone on a day when so many received news of loved ones not returning home. I basked in the afterglow of the incredible outcome for this family.

Before we ended our shift of 12 hours in the daylight of a new morning, we made it a point to seek out Sergeant Mitch.

"Don't worry," he responded. "I'll make good on my promise."

Later, he did—with an awesome commendation and a steak dinner to boot.

Mrs. B wrote a letter to the mayor of Los Angeles, resulting in a mayoral commendation for both Godinez and me.

Mr. and Mrs. B persevered through their imprisonment during WWII. Perhaps that same tenacity kept them holding on that night, refusing to let go of hope. Almost 30 years later, that lesson remains rooted in my heart and mind—a lesson I hope to remember forever.

As I reflected on that night and the commendations going forward, the one thing that continued to replay in my head came from my academy drill instructor. Todd's voice saying, "You never quit. Never."

We didn't quit, Todd. We never quit.

The Day We Cornered OJ

June 17, 1994 dawned with the same news on every radio and television station. OJ Simpson.

Suspected of killing Nicole Simpson and Ron Goldman, the LAPD expected his surrender before noon. The two victims still lay inside the LA Coroner's Office, awaiting the forensic posts. The story was the talk of the town. Hell, it was the talk of the world. A super athlete loved by most people accused of double murder? Of course, everyone talked about it.

Everyone expected OJ to surrender peacefully, and we had nothing to do with his arrest since another precinct planned for him to go there. We learned he didn't show up, but none of the high-ranking officers had a clue to his whereabouts. Not much we could do about it anyway—unless he showed up in our neighborhood.

I was working the streets of the West Los Angeles Division, commonly referred to as WLA. We always had action in this division, bordering Wilshire Division, Pacific Division, and Parts of West Valley Division. Ranging from homicides, bank robberies, drive-by shootings, carjackings, rape—the list goes on.

No safe haven in this area. We always caught a "Hot Call" to roll on.

That day, I was working overtime with my partner Kelly Chrisman. Kelly was a tenured police officer who came from a movie-star family. A great man and a great partner you could always count on. I never minded patrolling with Chrisman.

After we loaded up our black and white patrol car, Kelly asked, "Hey, Jimbo, need to do anything? I'm hungry. Let's get a bite to eat before it gets busy."

I had no problem with that. "Great. But can we go to the Schwinn bike shop first? I bought two bikes for my kids."

"Sure. Let's go, partner."

We got into our 1988 Chevrolet Impala and headed toward Pico Blvd. to pick up the bikes. I couldn't wait to give them to my kids.

Inside the store, I was paying for the bikes while Kelly waited inside the door.

Kelly yelled across the shop. "Jimbo, we gotta go. The dispatcher is clearing us to head to Rockingham."

OJ lived on Rockingham. His house?

He continued. "OJ is on the freeway heading toward West LA."

I was walking these two bikes out of the shop, trying to cram them in the back seat of the black and white, which was a pain in the ass. With the cage that separated the officers from any prisoner you would place in the back seat, a pair of bikes barely fit.

After finally getting the bikes in the back, Kelly blurted, "We can't leave these in the car. Do you have a truck or something?"

"Yeah, I have an open bed Toyota, but they won't be secure." I couldn't afford for the bikes to disappear.

Although sympathetic to my concerns, Kelly shot straight with me. "Then that's where they need to go. Sorry."

We raced to the officers' off-site parking for West LA Division, put the bikes in the back of the truck bed, said a prayer they'd still be there later, and raced to the Rockingham address using a code 3—lights and siren.

Approaching 6:00 p.m., we approached the address. As we neared a freeway overpass at Pico Blvd. and the 405 Freeway, people jumped over the barrier walls onto the actual freeway, sticking their heads out to view the pursuit.

"This is fucking nuts, Jimbo. Look at these fucking people," Kelly yelled above the screaming siren of our patrol car.

He laid on the horn several times as people darted on foot in front of our vehicle.

We both yelled out the window. "Get the fuck out of the way!"

As the passenger, I navigated for Kelly, trying to make sure we didn't hit any people or other vehicles. "Kelly, clear right, go! Clear left, go!" We busted through red traffic control lights, praying drivers stopped.

The intensity of Kelly's driving was textbook. Everything we learned as Los Angeles Police Officers in the police academy played out that evening—our finest hour. Surreal. We were going to OJ Simpson's house.

When we rolled into the area of

Rockingham, we killed our lights and siren. SWAT Sergeant Charlie Duke flagged us down.

We pulled up next to Sgt. Duke. "Where you want us?"

"Guys, take the black and white and block the back gate. Then take a position of cover across the street."

"You got it, sir."

Grimness covered Duke's face. "If he blasts out that gate with the Bronco, disable it with your Ithaca."

Sgt. Duke referred to our Ithaca Model 37 12-gauge pump shotgun. He didn't intend to play around despite the celebrity of our alleged suspect.

By that time, the noise in the area grew intense. Approaching police sirens, police and news helicopters flying overhead, people shouting—all of it deafening. A SWAT sniper dressed in a Ghillie suit scrambled up a palm tree in the center of OJ's yard, his rifle slung over his back. The suit blended into the tree, leaving him well hidden from anyone who didn't know his position.

The sergeant instructed us to be on Simplex on our radios, allowing us to talk back and forth with each other, but dispatch couldn't hear our transmissions.

Sgt. Duke addressed the sniper. "If OJ runs for a touchdown, take him down."

"Roger that." The sniper moved his rifle to a ready position, intent on taking a shot if necessary.

Kelly held his place of cover, close enough I would normally hear him without any effort. With all the noise in the area, he shouted, and I barely made out his words. "Jimbo, you believe this shit?"

"It's nuts, Kelly. This is so nuts! Are you ready, brother?"

"I'm ready, Jimbo. I'm ready." Kelly crouched behind a brick mailbox, waiting at full alert.

I followed his lead and took cover behind one too, choosing to take a seated position. I leveled that Ithaca shotgun from my place near the rear gate. Kelly perched across from me, maybe 25 feet, with his Beretta model 92FS department issued 9 mm at the ready position.

Police sirens wailed, growing louder. Helicopter rotors throbbed against the air, the repeated rhythm so intense my head buzzed.

Adrenaline pumping through my veins, I stayed focused on the task at hand despite the skull-shattering noise. The Ithaca up, tight against my shoulder, I waited. Anticipation put me on edge, as I willed myself to remain steady.

"Be ready," I kept telling myself.

"Jimbo, they're getting close." Kelly yelled toward my direction, never shifting his eyes off the gate.

"Roger, brother. I'm ready." Training kicked in, my breathing calmed, and I reset the shotgun, hoping I didn't need it, but prepared with my entire being if I did.

The sirens kept getting louder and louder.

"Shit! They're almost here," one officer reported over the radio.

Sgt. Duke's calm voice came across the radio. "All perimeter units, get ready. They are approaching our location. Be aware of any crossfire and stay in your positions."

This was it. All our training took over, steadying our nerves for whatever came next.

A moment later, patrol cars with lights blazing and sirens screaming pulled into the front driveway area of OJ Simpson's house on Rockingham.

The noise, loud earlier, resounded through the neighborhood, roaring so intently I thought my ears might burst.

Whoop, Whoop, Whoop.

Several patrol cars stopped, the sounds growing more raucous by the moment. My head pulsed with pain, more intense than anything I ever experienced before that night.

"Stay focused Jim. Eyes on the target. Remember what you were told to do." If I repeated the words to myself enough, I'd take care of business. I swallowed hard, waiting to see how the night unfolded.

Then, without fanfare, there came the white Ford Bronco followed by several police cars from various jurisdictions. California Highway Patrol, Orange County Sheriffs, San Diego County Sheriffs, LAPD, and finally the Bronco pulled into the driveway.

Whoop, whoop, whoop, whoop.

"Damn it! Turn off your sirens." Not sure if I said the words or merely thought them with my buzzing head. They must have heard me.

The sirens went silent while officers shouted, "Turn off the truck! Let us see your hands!"

Perfect protocol for attempting to make a felony stop. The occupants didn't cooperate. Stillness fell over the area. Everyone waiting, anticipating what might happen next. A collective holding of breaths as we wondered. How would this end?

Sgt. Duke's voice quietly addressed us. "All units, maintain positions."

We readjusted, pressing weapons tighter, ready for anything.

"We are in contact with the driver," Sgt. Duke relayed. Although we breathed a bit easier, we remained at a ready position, aware the entire scenario could go south—quickly.

We found out later the driver was a friend of Simpson's.

Everything quietened. Only one voice rang through the night air, instructing the occupants to step out of the truck. "You will not be hurt." Over and over, this male voice continued with the assurance of safety for the Bronco occupants.

This went on for what seemed like an eternity as we all held our positions, still ready to move. Only the roar of helicopter rotor blades above us filled the air. Blue and red lights flashed, visible all the way down Rockingham. The area settled into a dreamlike state, appearing almost normal—except for helicopters, flashing lights, and a small army of law enforcement.

At long last, the occupants stepped out of the Bronco. Simpson surrendered and Los Angeles SWAT cuffed and detained him. We all breathed, a silent collective release of tension.

Supervisors instructed us to stay in the area and maintain the perimeter, allowing nobody in other than police personnel. Crowds gathered outside our perimeter. Several LAPD officers, including Kelly and me, had to maintain the area. Some citizens from all over started pushing and shoving, demanding to enter the area.

Let me put it in a nice way. They did not enter the area. Not on our watch!

Another patrol unit relieved us in the early morning hours. Kelly Chrisman and I, hot, sweaty and exhausted, moved our black and white patrol car that blocked OJ Simpson's back gate. We turned the key on the Chevrolet Impala and left the area.

The entire way out, common citizens who

wanted in the area so badly shouted as we passed. "You fucking pigs. Fuck you. Let us in you fucking pigs."

Unbelievable. We did our jobs, aiding in the arrest of a double homicide suspect, and withstood the abuse from people who most likely didn't know OJ personally. Had it been any other person, would the people be there? Would they even care?

As we drove by, we waved at them and said, "Hi."

Under our breaths, we spoke our minds. "Get out of the way you motherfuckers."

Kelly looked at me. "This shit is unbelievable, Jimbo. This is something we will be able to tell our kids—hell even our grandkids."

"I hear ya, brother. Let's get the heck outta here and go home."

As we pulled into the West LA Police Station officers' parking, which is just adjacent to the front door of the station, my white Toyota pickup truck waited.

Kelly blurted, "Jimbo, I see your kids' bikes. Holy shit! They're still there."

"Praise God!" I boomed. "Let's go home,

my friend. Let's go home."

We cleared over the radio. "8X57. Show us end of watch."

"Roger 8X57," responded the dispatcher. "Goodnight."

Plane Crash — Pacific Division

During 1994, I was working for the Los Angeles Police Department assigned out of the West Los Angeles Division. On a July night that year, I worked a mid-pm watch under the call sign of 8X68. Our duty hours ran from 1830 to 0330 hours. I was assigned a brand-new rookie that graduated from the academy one month prior. Officer Terr was a very young and ambitious rookie with a great personality and the willingness to learn.

I introduced Officer Terr to the beat area where we provided coverage, explaining our main goal — cover the area when a shift 2A Car (2-person car) went down, busy with a radio call, booking a prisoner, or maybe taking their lunch break.

We picked up several calls in the area, staying relatively busy.

Terr said, "I never realized this shift does so much."

"Yup. We back up the entire area, even though we are assigned this beat. We go everywhere if we have to."

"That's cool."

I smiled, glad he found it cool, but I kept my thoughts tucked inside. Young at 21 years of age, I had a good 10 years on the rookie, and covering a large area didn't always feel pleasant.

At around 1900 hours, we heard a Pacific Division Sergeant over the radio putting out a help call in his area of 2900 Barrington. The Sergeant advised that a plane crashed in a residential area on Barrington.

I saw a lot of things in my job. A plane crash fell way beyond ordinary.

"Shit, Terr. Let's go! Advise that we are responding code 3."

"Roger 8X68, responding to Barrington." Dispatch would relay to the sergeant.

Flipping on lights and siren, we headed that direction, only a mile away. Smoke rose in the air, guiding us straight to the crash.

"8X68. Show us code 6 at the Barrington

location."

"Roger 8X68."

We rolled into the location and immediately took a position to block traffic on the roadway before vaulting from the cruiser.

Shit, we beat the fire department here.

Only three cars were on scene when we arrived—the Pacific Division sergeant, a Pacific Division beat car, and us. We ran toward the house alongside the two Pacific officers, uncertain what to expect.

Within seconds, the house came into view. A single-engine plane crashed, the nose penetrating the front exterior. The rest of the plane lay tail down in the front yard. Smoke billowed and rose from the wreckage, flames licking the plane and home. The closer we moved to the plane, the more it pushed us back. Smoke stole my breath. Heat, intense. Still no fire department. Watching in shock, it seemed like hours passed, but only minutes later, LAFD arrived.

The Pacific Division Sergeant yelled, "Get back! This thing might blow. One last attempt. Get in there and help the pilot out." He glanced over at us. "I told you both to get back. Now get back, damn it."

He didn't have to tell us again.

As we backed off several yards, mind-blowing screams drifted over the roar of fire, sirens, and all the other noises.

"Help me! Help me! I'm burning in here." The pilot continued screaming while the LAFD worked to extinguish the fire.

I glanced over at Officer Terr, tears trickling down his face. I blinked my eyes, controlling my emotions as best I could. The pilot's cries tore at my heart.

"Shit, Terr, there's nothing we can do brother."

"I know, I know." He wiped his face. "Jim, that guy's gonna die, isn't he?"

"Probably so." I placed a hand on his shoulder. "Terr, we tried, but we would've put ourselves in peril if we continued moving forward. You know that."

"I know. I'm just sick to my stomach."

My belly roiled in sympathy.

We stayed on the scene for several hours to assist Pacific Division with traffic control and interview witnesses until more help arrived. The sergeant thanked us for responding.

"Hey, we are all blue here. We will always help," I said.

"Thank you, brothers." He looked straight into my eyes, a soft glow in his. "Be safe guys." We shook hands and left.

Terr and I went to a local gas station to wash our faces and hands. Crud filled the air at the crash site, ending up on our clothes, faces, and hands.

For the first hour, back in our patrol car, quietness fell over our West Los Angeles Division, which was odd. The two of us echoed the silence. We drove around looking for possible criminal activity in our beat.

Nothing.

Finally, I pulled into a parking lot, killed the lights, and looked at Terr.

"Wanna talk about what we just did?"

He took a deep breath. "That was disturbing to me. Especially when that guy started screaming that he was on fire."

"I know. Me too." I sighed. "We are out here to help the public, but unfortunately this time we weren't able to do that. Terrible situation. It tears me up too, but we tried our best without putting our lives in jeopardy. We couldn't save him, no matter how hard we tried. If we had a chance to get him out alive, it'd be worth the risk, but we can't sacrifice ourselves."

"I know you're right, but it still bothers me."

Not long after that, we called in our Code 7 (lunch break). Most of the time, we chatted while eating. That night, we both kept quiet, trying to enjoy our dinner. Down deep, the earlier events wore heavy on both of us, the screams for help lingering in our memories.

As the years passed, I experienced times when memories from my police department days arise for whatever reason. Some situations trigger those moments. The scenes involving me and my partners rake through my brain. The crash scene lingers, forever etched in my mind.

I tell myself we did our very best that night, and we did. Like we say in police work, I compartmentalized the horrific visions that replayed then and sometimes even now. I moved forward after that night, knowing we did our best against a beast we couldn't defeat.

Reflections

Being a police officer requires the ability to handle all situations. Some are hard to do, wrenching the heart with pain no one wants to see or ever endure.

Throughout my career, my job required death notifications to surviving members of a family—a wife, husband, grandparents, or children of the deceased. By no means did I find this part of my job an easy feat. I wouldn't wish that responsibility on anyone, but unfortunately, it went with the job.

To this day, I still see faces of the deceased, etched in my mind, along with the survivors I had to tell. It's truly amazing—dealing with such horror and weird situations in my career that I am somewhat normal and didn't turn into a person with substance abuse issues.

Although I'm sure I had PTSD, it has since

faded over the years I've been gone. My wife tells me I ground my teeth every night back then.

We didn't go around spreading joy to people in the middle of the night. Someone dressed in a police uniform, knocking on your door or ringing the doorbell at all different times of the day—never meant something good. Difficult for me as an officer, horrendous for the ones on the other side of the door.

During my career as a police officer, people answered. They stood there, staring at me for a moment, only to slam the door in my face. They knew I brought bad news, and some people didn't want to hear what they expected to come from my mouth. Others cried hysterically. A few wanted to hit us, in denial that something happened to their loved one. We took the abuse, imagining the emotions filling them, never holding a bereaved person responsible for the momentary lack of self-control.

Death notifications take on new meaning for a person in this line of work. I know it did for me. For a difficult minute, hour, or day, I sympathized with the people we notified. While some of the notifications came for families of criminals, they still hurt. Many times, the death happened through accidents or natural causes. None of that mattered in the brief time when we spoke with the loved ones. The reason didn't ease the pain or shock.

As an officer, I faced an uncomfortable moment, then I got to walk away. Secretly, we hoped never to know by experience how those people crumbled inside, yet always fearing someday we might.

Fast forward to July 2012. I had retired and moved from California to Texas.

At 1:30 a.m., my wife and I both woke to a ringing phone. The display showed our daughter Stephanie's cell phone number—a parent's worst way to wake from sound sleep. Groggy, still half asleep, I answered, expecting my daughter's voice.

A male voice screamed over the phone. Confused, I shot up in bed, recognizing her boyfriend's voice.

He screamed frantically. "Stephanie passed out. She's turning blue."

My head cleared. I entered emergency mode. "Have you started CPR?"

"I don't know how." Sobs choked his voice.

Don't freak out. "Calm down. I'll walk you through it." I kept my voice even. Went through each step for CPR, praying he did it.

Suddenly, he blurted, "The paramedics just arrived."

OK. At least he called 911. Good. She'll be alright.

With my wife's hand on my arm, I held my breath for what seemed like hours. Minutes later, in reality, I dared breathe. The medics got her heart going again and were transporting her to the emergency room.

My wife and I lunged out of bed and threw on clothes.

"Let's go." I didn't want to wait one more second.

Our daughter lived over 35 miles away from us. The hospital they were taking her to was close to her apartment. I was doing over 100 MPH on the toll road. I couldn't get to our precious child fast enough. As a father, a parent, that's what we do for our children. We had to reach her.

When we arrived, we ran into the ER. They were moving Stephanie to ICU. She lay on a gurney, her eyes somewhat open.

My wife and I flanked her and ran alongside the gurney, grasping at her arms. "Mom and Dad are here, sweetie. Hold on. Stay with us."

I'd uttered those words before as a cop. But that was my child. Not the same.

They took her into the ICU. Her body temperature raged. Much too high.

"We need to cool her down with cool packs." The ER doctor was a joke. Constantly rubbing his face, it looked like the guy's sleep was interrupted.

I have been in a whole lot of emergency rooms in my career. I knew a read on condition ASAP was critical.

The doctor dragged his heels, as if he had no clue what to do next.

My temper flared. "Let's go! What are we doing here?"

The doctor rubbed his face again. "I don't know how long she's been down. I'm trying to find a neurologist on call to check her out."

"Look, get one, and get it now. We need to medivac her out of here to a better trauma center."

"I can't do that."

The papa bear in me wanted to throw the doctor across the room. That wouldn't help Stephanie. He couldn't get a medivac, but I could. Before he opened his mouth again, I was on the phone with my friends at CareFlite.

The CEO of CareFlite, Jim Swartz, made sure a helicopter came to our location immediately. In a matter of minutes, I am here to tell you that chopper was on the hospital roof, rotor blades turning. The paramedic crew took over, getting Stephanie hooked up, on a stretcher, aboard the helicopter, and off to a trauma center.

Upon landing, the hospital staff met them on their roof, rushing her inside. The doctor on call was right there. Checking out the situation. Calling out what he needed. Much more than what I saw from that so-called doctor at the original ER, rubbing his eyes and face continuously.

Stephanie was in the ICU at the trauma center for five days. The doctors all stated that she was starting to show improvement. Her cardiac doctor had concerns that she at the least needed a pacemaker because they hit her with electric shocks to restart her heart multiple times.

The neurologist voiced concerns because she had not woken up yet. Normally, within three days, he told us, patients start to move and wake up. She had done neither.

The doctors ordered a test with dye placed intravenously in her arm. With a scan, they could then observe the dye's flow and how it traveled through her body's functions.

Like I mentioned earlier, when someone approaches you, one look at their facial expression reveals it's not good news.

The doctor looked at my wife and me. I knew it wasn't good.

"The dye flowed perfectly through her body but stopped right at her neck. I'm sorry. Your daughter lacked blood flow to her brain for too long." Compassion shone in the doctor's eyes. "She has no brain function. I am so sorry. I wish there was something else we could do."

Our whole world fell apart. We lost our beautiful daughter. What now? Confusion set in for us. We weren't supposed to deal with this for our child, were we?

I knew better—having been the one telling a parent their child was gone. But it never prepared me to hear those words about my daughter. It didn't matter that they came from a doctor instead of a police officer. The finality of it shattered my heart.

Earlier, I shared that when making notifications to families as a police officer, I could just walk away. Back then, I did my best to show compassion in those moments and hoped I offered some comfort in a split second that changed a family's life forever. Some of those times touched me more than others, but in the end, I walked away and went home to my wife and children.

We cannot walk away. This time, the notification came for us, and it's forever for my wife, for me, and for our other children.

Stephanie was a graduate of Texas A&M, a teacher in Richardson, Texas where she was a sixth-grade reading teacher for students in a Title 1 school setting. Many of the children came from single-family homes with only a mother or a grandparent who took care of them.

Our daughter relentlessly made sure her students got an equitable education. She tutored them before and after school. She bought them food, clothes, and school supplies. Our angel made sure her students were successful in whatever they wanted to do in life. She encouraged them to go to college and taught them they could do anything if they worked hard enough!

Stephanie died suddenly on July 25, 2012 at 26 years old. Her time on Earth ended at such a young age. In many ways, Stephanie attained the change she sought to achieve, but she was never able to experience fully what every teacher hopes for their pupils. Stephanie's life fell short of witnessing her students conquer college, transition into adulthood, and lead an impactful, productive life.

Although she is no longer with us, the principles Stephanie believed in will always remain timeless.

∞∞∞∞∞∞

To continue with our daughter's legacy and memory, we established the Stephanie Lynne Calams Memorial Scholarship Foundation. We continue honoring her by helping those who need assistance. The Stephanie Lynne Calams Memorial Scholarship keeps her dream alive where it mattered to her most—the school she taught at and the city she lived in. Her memory will carry on where she left off and continue to instill the values Stephanie held so high.

The funds raised for her foundation assist students, enabling them to attend college or a technical school by helping with their finances. The proceeds from this book will go toward assisting students in need from a Title 1 school setting nationally.

The Stephanie Lynne Memorial Scholarship Foundation is a 501(c)3 organization.

For more information about Stephanie and her story, or to make donations, visit www.stephaniescholarship.org.

∞∞∞∞∞∞∞

Stephanie had the biggest heart, always giving and never taking. We miss her—so very much.

God Bless our Angel Stephanie—always.

References

California Department of Conservation. (2007, February
        1). *Northridge Earthquake, January 17, 1994.*
        Retrieved July 5, 2021, from CA.gov:
        https://www.conservation.ca.gov/cgs/earthqua
        kes/northridge

Writer, S. (2020, April 15). *How Often Do Earthquakes
        Happen in California.* Retrieved July 5, 2021,
        from Reference:
        https://www.reference.com/science/earthquak
        es-happen-california-5a793271bd53fb9a

About the Author

Jim Calams is a tenured police officer with over 23 years of experience having worked for the Maricopa County Sheriff's Office, Phoenix Police Department, and the Los Angeles Police Department. His career included assignments in Patrol, Special Problems Unit, Gang Unit, and Community Relations. Jim resides in the Great State of Texas with his wife D'Ann, living his best life with his children and grandchildren.

Made in the USA
Las Vegas, NV
27 December 2021

39343340R00085